Healthy Volunteers in Commercial Clinical Drug Trials

Shadreck Mwale

Healthy Volunteers in Commercial Clinical Drug Trials

When Human Beings Become Guinea Pigs

palgrave
macmillan

Shadreck Mwale
School of Applied Social Sciences
University of Brighton
Brighton, UK

ISBN 978-3-319-59213-8 ISBN 978-3-319-59214-5 (eBook)
DOI 10.1007/978-3-319-59214-5

Library of Congress Control Number: 2017943647

Printed on acid-free paper

This Palgrave Macmillan imprint is published by Springer Nature
The registered company is Springer International Publishing AG
The registered company address is: Gewerbestrasse 11, 6330 Cham, Switzerland

Moriah and Jesse
For always reminding what is really important in life

Acknowledgements

First and foremost, I owe my biggest debt to writing this book to my participants,- who took the time to share their experiences and stories on their journeys as human guinea pigs. You challenged me and opened my eyes to the hidden world of human involvement in clinical trials. THANK YOU very much.

Thanks to my colleagues at University of Brighton, Ms. Marylynn Fyvie-Gauld, Dr. Kepa Artaraz, Dr. Mark Erickson, Prof. Phil Haynes, and my mentor Prof. Gillian Bendelow, for your unwavering support and for giving me pause for thought at different stages of putting this book together. I am also grateful to Dr. Sindi Gordon University of Sussex, for her creative writing input, and to Dr. Simon Lewis, for always providing critical feedback on clinical trial processes and practices.

Thanks also to my supervisors Dr. Catherine Will and Dr. Alex Faulkner, both at University of Sussex, for your support.

I am grateful to all the reviewers, and to the editorial team at Palgrave, Holly Tyler and Jo O'Neill, for the feedback and for taking me to task on various oddities to help me tighten my argument throughout the process of putting this book together.

Last, but not least, the research on which this book is based was funded by the ESRC; thanks for what was a life-changing financial support.

Disclaimer: All names of research participants used in this publication have been replaced with fictitious names to protect their identities. Any resemblance to real persons, living or dead, is purely coincidental.

Contents

Abbreviations

ABPI	Association of British Pharmaceutical Industry
CCRU	Common Cold Research Unit
CISCRP	Centre for Information and Study on Clinical Research Participation
CRO	Contract Research Organisation
FDA	Food and Drug Administration
GP	General Practitioners
HV	Healthy Volunteer
ICH	International Conference on Harmonisation
MHRA	Medicines and Healthcare products Regulatory Agency
NHS	National Health Service
ONS	Office of National Statistics
REC	Research Ethics Committee
TB	Tuberculosis
TGN	TeGeNero
TOPS	The Over-Volunteering Prevention Strategy
WHO	World Health Organisation

List of Tables

Introduction

Every time I met participants for an interview in central London around lunchtime, it was incredibly difficult to find a suitable place and space. On this particular occasion, after a few minutes wandering the streets, the interviewee and I settled on a pub not far from the Tube station and close enough to her next appointment. Settling down with coffee, we talked about life, what she had studied, what work she had done, and where she was now. Then, we came down to one of the core questions for the meeting. 'Why clinical drug trials? Why not another job?' I queried. Her response was unusual, and it changed how I saw myself as a researcher and my approach to the subject I was exploring. She replied:

> Look at me. By now [at this stage in my life], I should have a well-paid job, a house, and a good car, but I don't…and I am a graduate [master's degree graduate]. (Sasha, female, 27)

The invitation 'look at me' can have many meanings. At one extreme, it could be an invitation to pity someone, while on the other it could be showing off, meaning 'See how successful or good I am'? In between these extremes, the invitation 'look at me' is not a call to see or gaze at the person in front of you; rather, it invites one to see the common sense of justice and entitlement we all share. It speaks of our sense of (in)justice, in relation to what we feel we deserve or not. Where this sense of justice or injustice comes from is another discussion but, simply put, one could argue it derives from our own socially and culturally prescribed expectations of our lives. However, often when we are in a position of relative privilege, when discussions of injustice and inequality are brought up, it is easy to forget the impact these disadvantages have on people's lives in general. In this context, inequality and disadvantage can easily be interpreted as something that happens to others or indeed only affects other people and not us, or, indeed, that they deserve what happens to them. We can easily see ourselves as not part of the conversation or not part of the issues, as we are not affected. Thus, we can distance ourselves from any consideration and discussion of such issues.

However, the invitation 'look at me' is also a bidding, inviting us to see how interconnected we all are. It invites us to look beyond the class, racial, gender, and other differences we think exist among people in society and begin to see how connected we are with those we otherwise see as the 'other'. Public and academic debates of human involvement in clinical drug trials, specifically healthy volunteering, conjure images of people in certain situations,—homeless, poor, uneducated, among others—as volunteers. In doing so, whether intentionally or unintentionally, we see ourselves as unaffected, and thus not part of the conversation of healthy volunteer involvement in clinical drug trials. In the words of the philosopher Simone Weil '"…You do not interest me…". No man (I add: or woman) can say these words to another without committing a cruelty and offending against injustice' (Weil 1977, 313). In other words, when we distance ourselves from conversations on healthy volunteering, we are saying these peoples' lives do not concern us. When such views are coupled with the Western sociopolitical tendency to overemphasise individual choice and rights, it becomes even more justifiable and acceptable to see healthy volunteers as the 'other' (Spivak 1985), and yet capable, rational individuals who are thus responsible for the consequences of their actions. However, seeing healthy volunteering purely through the lens of rights and choice obscures inequality and the ethical questions regarding human involvement in such trials. To consider healthy volunteering as not our concern is to ignore how inequality is experienced and perpetuated in everyday life.

Nonetheless, we all benefit from healthy volunteering in clinical drug trials. We all use pharmaceutical products or medicines in one form or another, products which were once tested on healthy subjects who risked their lives. To that end, we are all connected, whether as volunteers, users, or indeed as professionals who mediate public use of medicines.

Therefore, we all are inevitably part of the conversation on healthy volunteer involvement in clinical drug trials. The invitation 'look at me' is a bid for us all to pause and reflect on who exactly are healthy volunteers. Why are financial rewards on offer in clinical drug trials attractive to some people? Why do healthy volunteers have to resort to clinical drug trials—as shown in Abadie's (2010) work on healthy volunteers as professional guinea pigs in the US—to make a living?

Guinea pigs are cute animals, but the term "guinea pigs" to refer to humans in experimental contexts is interesting. It presages risk, power, experimentation, inexperience, and possibly images of laboratories among others. The origin of the phrase referring to human involvement in experiments is unclear; however, references to humans as guinea pigs in an experiment can be seen in eighteenth century literature. Specifically, it referred to men from Guinea in the West African region (from which the rodents are thought to have originated), who were involved in shipping in the routes between West Africa, South America, and Southern Europe. It was during this period that the rodents we now call guinea pigs were introduced to Europe, mostly by Spanish sailors (Adam 2006). However, reference to inexperience and naivety to describe persons as guinea pigs as mentioned earlier can be found in *The Adventures of a Kidnapped Orphan*, (1747; 69):

> He sent his nephew, at the age of fourteen, on a voyage as a Guinea pig.

Even then, the phrase did not have the experimental connotations it has today. The link between the term 'guinea pig' and experiments developed in the twentieth century. In the early twentieth century, following the introduction of the rodents into Europe, scientists discovered some biological similarities between humans and guinea pigs. Since then, it has become common practice to use guinea pigs in experiments. For instance, German scientist Robert Koch used guinea pigs to establish that *Mycobaterium tuberculosis* causes tuberculosis (TB) (Adam 2006). The most direct link to the use of the term 'guinea pig' to refer to experimentation derives from the writings of George Bernard Shaw, who was what we would now call an animal rights activist, and a vegetarian. Shaw was appalled by the use of animals in experiments justified by claims that such research would transform human society. In *The Quintessence of Ibsenism* (1913; 105) Shaw writes

'The… folly which sees in the child nothing more than the vivisector sees in a guinea pig: something to experiment on with a view to rearranging the world.'

Since then, the term 'guinea pig' became established to refer to the practice of subjecting humans to experiments. Today, within the social sciences Tishler and Bartholomae (2003), Elliot (2008), and Abadie (2010) among others, have used this phrase to point to the exploitation of marginalised, mostly ethnic minority men, in commercial clinical drug trials in the US. In this book, I use the term 'guinea pig' in reference to the ethical and sociopolitical challenges associated with subjecting humans to medical research, and the need for a reflection on issues affecting those who come forward to act as guinea pigs.

Drawing on qualitative research data from a survey of 187 healthy volunteers and in-depth interviews with 35 healthy volunteers, eight regulatory officials, and four professionals from the contract research organisations (CRO), this book aims to present an account of healthy volunteer involvement in clinical drug trials in the UK. In the following chapters, I argue for a view of healthy volunteering that problematizes volunteering by going beyond the discourse of right and choice to consider the complex situations that make healthy people become human guinea pigs. The title of the book sums up the general need to recognise the politics and ethical challenges of healthy volunteer involvement in clinical drug trials. It also points to the need for a nuanced understanding of healthy volunteering by considering the hidden relationships between social inequality, health, and clinical drug trials and how they make guinea pigging a viable option for some people.

References

Abadie, R. (2010). *The professional guinea pig: Big pharma and the risky world of human subjects*. London: Duke University Press.

Adam, D. (2006). Why use guinea pigs in animal testing? *The Guardian, The Science Behind the News*. Available at https://www.theguardian.com/science/2005/aug/25/thisweekssciencequestions1

Elliott, C. (2008). Guiea-pigging, Healthy human subjects for drug-safety trials are in demand. But is it a living?. *The New Yorker*. Available at http://www.newyorker.com/magazine/2008/01/07/guinea-pigging.

Spivak, G. C. (1985). The Rani of Sirmur: An essay in reading the archives. *History and Theory, 24*(3), 247–272.

Tishler, C. L., & Bartholomae, S. (2003). Repeat participation among normal healthy research volunteers: Professional guinea pigs in clinical trials? *Perspectives in Biology and Medicine, 46*(4), 508–520.

Weil, S. (1977). *The Simone Weil reader.* New York: Dorset Press, University of Michigan.

CHAPTER 1

Healthy Volunteering and Phase I Clinical Drug Trials in the UK

Abstract This chapter introduces the rationale, context, and main themes of the book. It explores what clinical drug trials are and why a sociological analysis of human involvement is important. It provides a context of human involvement in clinical drug trials; this includes a discussion on the history of human involvement and interrogation of the volunteer as a concept. This chapter charts the changes to regulatory frameworks and how they brought about the shift from the use of captive populations to 'volunteers' capable of rational consent. It also includes a discussion on the commercial contexts in which clinical drug trials take place today.

Keywords Clinical drug trials · Healthy volunteers · Volunteering
Phase I

Beyond the Veil of Choice and Consent

Asha, at the time a recent migrant from Eastern Europe, had come into the UK with the help of her then 'boyfriend'. After a few weeks together in the UK, the boyfriend started to talk of the need to make money to survive. This was a concern she shared, but for her, the solution was finding a job. The boyfriend suggested healthy volunteering. She said:

S. Mwale, *Healthy Volunteers in Commercial Clinical Drug Trials*,
DOI 10.1007/978-3-319-59214-5_1

> I had never heard or thought of clinical drug trials as a way of making money until then. (Asha, female, 29)

Worried about the risks of being a guinea pig, Asha refused to take part in clinical drug trials. Nevertheless, her boyfriend ignored her, taking advantage of the fact that Asha was new to the country, and unbeknownst to the research team and everyone else at the time, registered her, took her to the clinical trial units for assessments and admissions, waited each time, and picked her up on the last day of the clinical trial. Asha said, 'It was worse when he actually boasted of having friends in the police, so I accepted to do it', though obviously very reluctantly. 'I was scared, very scared for my life but I could not talk to anyone about it, I feared for my life', she said, shaking her head. Surprisingly, Asha was forcibly enrolled into a clinical trial, not just once but on two different occasions and in two different clinical trial units. On both occasions, Asha was paid for her involvement in the trials, but she never saw the money she was paid and never told anyone about her ordeal. In her own words:

> Not that the money matters to me but it is just what this (being forced into taking part in clinical drug trials) has done to me…I am worried for my life and future health. (Asha, female, 29)

Asha's account demonstrates the problems of human involvement in clinical drug trials: choice and rational consent are overemphasised. This is because despite being under duress, within the confines of rational consent, Asha was officially eligible and a perfect candidate. These are some of the issues this book seeks to explore and state. My aim is to present experiences of healthy volunteers in clinical drug trials and their perception of attendant risks and rewards. I seek to demonstrate the role incentives play in healthy volunteer involvement in clinical drug trials and the ethical implications that financial rewards bring. This is because while there has been a lot of research on patient involvement in clinical drug trials in the UK (Featherstone and Donovan 2003; Hallowell et al. 2010), with the notable exception of Corrigan (2003) alone and with others, there has been little focus on healthy volunteers. Where healthy participants have been considered, it has been in combination with patient participants. This conflation suggests that the questions and even the ethical issues healthy volunteers face are the same as those patients face, when in fact they are not. This book therefore adds to the literature and debates on the ethics of human involvement in clinical drug trials by focusing solely on experiences of the healthy volunteer in the UK.

What are Clinical Drug Trials?

Clinical drug trials involve a set of studies that are required before new medicines are declared safe and effective for marketing. Relatively standardised across the globe, clinical drug trials are complex and elaborate processes carried out in several stages. This complexity contributes 'to the immense time, risk and expense of the drug development process' (Rajan 2006: 67). Initially, the drug goes through pre-clinical tests to evaluate toxicity. Pre-clinical testing usually involves conducting tests on animals to establish if the new drug is sufficiently safe to introduce into humans (Pocock 2000). If a drug is deemed too toxic, it does not proceed to the next stage; if considered sufficiently safe, it proceeds to clinical drug trials, which usually involves four stages, starting with the first-in-human phase or phase I.

This book focuses on phase I (first-in-human or phase I) clinical drug trials. These trials are drug trials carried out on a limited number of healthy volunteers with the aim of testing the basic safety of a newly developed Investigational Medicinal Product (IMP) and to determine the minimum and maximum dosages that can be administered without causing serious harm. The participants in this phase usually have no health benefits to gain from their involvement in these trials (Elliott and Abadie 2008; Goldacre 2012). It is worth noting that 'phase I clinical drug trials' can also refer to clinical drug trials that involve healthy participants on trials testing IMPs that are already on the market (Fisher 2015). Consequently, healthy volunteer experiences may differ depending on the type of phase I drug trial in which they are involved. Those based on newly developed IMPs are inherently riskier than those testing an existing licenced drug. In addition, some phase I drug trials are conducted on patients, particularly for cancer and HIV/AIDS drugs (Kohli-Laven et al. 2011). Strictly speaking, it is deemed unethical to expose healthy subjects to IMPs considered highly likely to be toxic to humans, although there are cases where such drugs have been tested on healthy subjects (Gupta et al. 2012; Guideline 2009).

Phase II trials involve a larger number of patients and aim to investigate further the efficacy and to determine the optimal dose. These trials involve patients in controlled numbers and hold no obvious benefits for participating patients (Pocock 2000). Phase III clinical drug trials involve samples of several thousand participants who are usually suffering from the disease for which the new drug has been developed. During phase III trials, the IMP continues to be tested for safety, but its therapeutic benefits are also evaluated. Phase IV trials aim at comparing existing remedies with the new drug and establishing how treatment might work in a broad range of patients (Kerr et al. 2006). Most drug compounds do not advance beyond phase I trials due to their toxicity. The process of taking an IMP from the laboratory to the market is also an arduous one, lasting between 10 and 15 years. Estimation of the real costs involved in this process is equally difficult. However, the process has become increasingly contentious as the public calls for cheaper drugs, arguing that production costs are low and that the market value that companies attach to the finished product is not justifiable (Abadie 2010).

Recently, phase I clinical drug trials have attracted public criticism following high-profile botched clinical drug trials. In Rennes, France in January 2016, one healthy volunteer died and a further four volunteers were left in critical condition after taking part in a phase I clinical drug trial for a drug to treat pain and mood disorders (Mwale 2016). While in London, UK, the Northwick Park incident of 2006, six healthy volunteers suffered severe side effects after taking part in a phase I trial for a cancer drug TGN 1412 (Hedgecoe 2013). Both these events have led to claims that the drug trials were conducted amid open disregard for safety and regulation. In the UK, there have been calls for tighter government regulation of the pharmaceutical industry, claiming that the regulatory framework favoured corporate interests over the safety and interests of participants (Stebbings et al. 2009). However, healthy volunteer involvement in clinical drug trials is not a new phenomenon.

Historical Context of Human Involvement in Clinical Drug Trials

Until the late 1930s, the production and use of medicines for humans was both uncontrolled and unconventional (Bartfai and Lees 2006). The development of the pharmaceutical industry as we know it today has its roots in major pharmacological developments and scientific breakthroughs that occurred before and after World War II, when antibiotics such as penicillin, streptomycin, and several other broad-spectrum antibiotics were discovered and mass-produced (Petryna and Kleinman 2006). Though drugs had been tested on people years before the late 1930s, the systematic testing of IMPs on humans is a recent phenomenon, and is connected to the rise of drug regulation and controls on how drugs can be administered (Bartfai and Lees 2006). Before the rise of drug regulation mechanisms, IMPs were tested haphazardly on patients, mostly vulnerable or captive populations such as prisoners and slaves; some of these practices continued even when a systematic procedure of drug testing developed in the twentieth century. In the United States, testing was carried out on prisoners, and in the UK on patients and army service personnel who served as human guinea pigs (Rosner 1996; Bolton 2005).

It was from the 1940s onwards that scientists started to test IMPs systematically on a few select individuals in randomised clinical drug trials (Marks 2009). The origin of systematic randomised clinical drug trials traces back to the Elixir Sulfanilamide tragedy of 1937[1] (Carpenter 2014). In the UK, up until the 1960s, drug developers were under no obligation to test or to demonstrate the safety of their drugs before marketing. The tragedy aroused widespread public disquiet over the safety of drugs. The U.S. Food and Drug Administration (FDA), at the time trying to establish itself as a force in regulating the industry, conducted an extensive investigation, which identified the lack of pre-marketing testing as a key precursor in the disaster. Therefore, on December 1, 1937, the legislation requiring drug manufacturers to provide'records of their clinical and non-clinical experiments' before drugs would be certified for marketing was amended (Carpenter 2014: 103). In the UK during this time, testing was voluntary; it was not until 1968 that systematic pre-marketing testing of IMPs was required (Rägo and Santoso 2008).

History of Healthy Volunteering: The 'Volunteering Turn'

The introduction of systematic testing of IMPs in 1968 was accompanied by changing attitudes to the use of human subjects in medical research following the landmark Nuremberg ruling. The development of the 1946 Nuremberg ruling followed revelations of grossly unethical research experiments in Nazi Germany in the 1940s, which eventually led to growing objections. The Nuremberg code on human involvement in clinical drug trials developed in response as a set of ethical codes of practice aimed at curbing the use of force and vulnerable captive populations in medical research (Scocoza 1989; Bartfai and Lees 2006). From here on the discourse of volunteering emerged, what I call the 'volunteering turn', as participants in clinical drug trials were now expected to be 'willing' and 'volunteers'.

However, policy responses to implementing drug testing and voluntarism in UK did not take place until post-1970s. A historical analysis by Hazelgrove (2002) show that the guidelines for voluntary recruitment of participants in clinical drug trials following the Nuremberg Code were largely ignored in the UK and the US. This neglect is illustrated in the thalidomide scandal of the 1950s onwards, when the anti-nausea drug was given marketing license despite its threat to public health (Hazelgrove 2002). Equally, Bolton (2005) shows that the use of soldiers and other army service personnel in testing was common practice at the time. Hazelgrove (2002) argues that the actions of Britain at the time of the Nuremberg Code served to divert attention away from its own unethical practices while ensuring the protection of professional power to carry out research. Reports by medical practitioners such as Pappworth (1967) exposed unethical practices in British hospital trials involving patients. During this period, self-experimentation was also common as researchers or staff in laboratories took part in their own studies. However, questions about risks and ethics are different when students in laboratories or patients in hospitals are asked by their lecturers and doctors, respectively, to take part in clinical drug trials. Here influence and power come into play as fears of letting superiors down may influence an individual's perception of risk and involvement in clinical drug trials (Goldacre 2012). Similarly, the works of Epstein and Washington on the post-Nuremberg history of clinical drug trials in the US show how 'captive' populations, e.g., prisoners, continued to be used well into the 1980s (Epstein 2004, 2008; Washington 2006). This practice was evident in the Tuskegee syphilis study in which black men were recruited through deception as subjects between 1931 and 1972 (Armstrong et al. 1999; Harris et al. 1996).

Conceptualising Volunteering

Having considered the historical background to human involvement in clinical drug trials, let's consider what the term 'volunteer' means. Within sociology, the term 'volunteer' is rarely discussed. In its daily use, volunteering presages willingness, help, and selfless acts without the prospect of payment. The term has long been open to interpretation; in general, it can be seen as doing something without being ordered or coerced, or expecting a reward; it is seen as a proactive rather than a reactive act (Wilson 2000). At the core of volunteering is the notion of freedom to act freely, in Berlin's (1958) terms of positive and negative freedom. For Berlin, negative freedom refers to the ability for individuals and groups to act as they can without interference. On the other hand, positive freedom refers to how individual actions are contoured by external forces. The criticisms of Berlin's views of freedom have been clearly outlined by many (Nelson 2005). With regards to healthy volunteers, while they are situated as capable of freely choosing to take part, one needs to consider how their actions are influenced by rewards on offer for volunteering. On the other hand, attention must be given to how acts of volunteering for certain groups tend to be more valued and deemed acceptable than others. For instance, among people in full-time employment, volunteering for a charity is a commendable thing to do. Historian Bolton (2005), observes that in the UK the term 'volunteer' is associated with the enlistment of soldiers during the world wars as the ultimate demonstration of courage and selflessness. Bolton argues that today volunteering seems to carry similarly loaded meanings. However, in the 1950s, particularly within the army, to volunteer came to be associated not only with a personal decision to enlist, but also with an expectation of service personnel to do certain things when asked and whenever the need arose. Within the army in the twentieth century, volunteering became synonymous with being 'committed'; today, it denotes willingness, kindness, and moral responsibility. Bolton illustrates the historical complexity of the term by citing an incident at the birth of the Common Cold Research Unit (CCRU) in the 1950s, when the management of the unit and the Ministry of Health at the time wanted to define the term 'volunteer'. In this exchange, the then Health Minister expressed concern over the use of prisoners and service personnel, considering them incapable of volunteering. Of interest, this shows how, even during the 1950s, officials indicated concern about using people who were not, strictly speaking, able to freely agree to participate in medical research because of the institutional context in which they may have perceived adverse consequences for failing to comply.

Within sociology, the term 'volunteer' is a contested concept. Wilson and Musick (1999) argue that volunteering can be informal or formal and can include productive work that should be recognised as requiring both social and cultural capital (Bourdieu 2005) to function; it should thus be rewarded. However, the reward here is not clearly defined; it could take the form of either money or nonmonetary rewards, such as encouragement or acknowledgement. Wilson (2000) argues that there is no consensus on the meaning of volunteering but that it can be linked to the giving of time freely to benefit others and is among a cluster of helping behaviours. In this case, the volunteer must be free, in Berlin's sense of negative freedom, and since the focus is on benefiting others, volunteers therefore must be altruistic. Other discussions in sociology about volunteering revolve around questions of motives, rationality, rewards, and altruism (Wuthnow 1993; Weber et al. 1963). However, less attention has been paid to the context in which volunteering takes place and the different meanings of volunteering in various social circumstances.

At the individual level, two theories of volunteering can be distinguished. The first considers the individual as complex, multi-dimensional, and located within a given context and background. This theory perceives volunteering subjectively and it emanates from sociological attempts to investigate motives for volunteering. The second theory assumes individuals are motivated by simple mechanisms; it considers the context in which decisions are made as complex, and is more behaviourist in orientation. This view also considers individuals as rational, thus accounts of volunteering are based on a cost-benefit analysis (Wilson 2000). However, for certain classes of people in society, the benefits to be gained from volunteering are so great for them that they outweigh the costs, even though these costs are so high that the 'average' person in that society would not even consider volunteering as an option. A person in that situation cannot truly be said to have volunteered, although they can be said to have chosen. In this book, I use a subjective approach to volunteering to consider not only the role of rewards and individual rationality, but also the conflicts and complexity of individuals as social actors and in social situations, and how these determine and define acts of voluntarism. There are arguments that in clinical drug trials, the concept of 'volunteering' is ideal as it relates to the communal and interdependent nature of everyday life (Geissler 2011). While ideas of volunteering as a social ideal are useful, one must consider how the social practice of volunteer is imbued with power which can be harnessed to influence definitions and acts of volunteering, as Asha's case in the opening sections of this chapter shows. Furthermore, volunteering can also be a political tool. For instance, in a 2014 UK government policy, to volunteer became linked with good citizenship; thus, a tool for distributing rights. In this policy context, welfare benefits of citizenship for those unable to work or unemployed are only to be available if they 'volunteer' to work (Department of Work and Pensions 2014). In addition, an advertisement on myukjobs.co.uk of 9th September 2013 featured a call for healthy volunteering as paid, permanent jobs. This demonstrates how 'to volunteer', particularly in clinical drug trials, cannot be taken uncritically. In some cases, to volunteer no longer means a willingness but a mandatory expectation to 'work' and 'contribute to society' to claim citizenship rights. This illustrates how certain groups have become targets for campaigns and policy action that essentially 'volunteer' them.

In this book, I use the term 'healthy volunteer', which is widely understood. My choice is not simply a matter of terminology, but also a preferred analytical framework referring to what might be termed the 'volunteering turn' following the Nuremberg ruling and subsequent legislation in which willingly consenting involvement became a guiding principle for human subject research. Firstly, the use of the term "healthy volunteer" distinguishes volunteering in clinical drug trials from other kinds of volunteering, such as those working in disasters (e.g., disease outbreaks), by clearly indicating that the discussion is concerned with volunteering in medical clinical drug trials. Secondly, when volunteering is associated with kindness and willingness to help others (Bolton 2005), it is likely to be considered in a way that is removed from the context of institutional power relations in which the volunteering acts take place. Hence, the aim here is to consider healthy volunteering by untangling the human subjects, institutions, and social circumstances (such as debt, unemployment, and homelessness) that are often taken for granted, as factors that shape and influence decisions, experiences, and perceptions of risk and subsequent volunteering. Healthy volunteering and the institutional contexts in which it occurs need to be brought together in an analytical dialogue because they are imbued with meaning and power, and influence each other (Sondhi 2013).

There is a need to consider how regulators, pharmaceutical corporations, and political and legislative bodies view healthy volunteers and shape their involvement in clinical drug trials. This context has been investigated by sociologists and anthropologists in the US. For instance, Epstein's (2008) sociological study on inclusion and politics of science and Fisher (2009) alone and with others sociological study on the economy of clinical drug trials in science and technology studies explored human involvement in such trials, looking at how both patients and healthy volunteers volunteer in clinical drug trials to access healthcare (Edelblute and Fisher 2015; Fisher and Kalbaugh 2011; Monahan and Fisher 2015). Note that these studies have been conducted in the US and emerging economies (Petryna's 2009; Rajan 2006), which have different social and political contexts from the UK. In focusing on the UK, the aim is to provide an understanding of human involvement in clinical drug trials in the national context.

Focusing on healthy volunteers also reveals the ambiguities of the institutional, social, and political contexts of low income, debt, and employment in which human involvement in clinical drug trials takes place. A healthy volunteer may be a willing participant but his or her motivation may be largely financial (Tishler and Bartholomae 2002). It should be noted, however, that in some contexts, for instance in the US, people take part in clinical drug trials as a means of accessing healthcare (Fisher 2009; Abade 2010). The healthy volunteer is actively involved in negotiating structures and institutional relations, rules, and influences that society may uncritically accept. Therefore healthy volunteers should be seen not just as human subjects, but as individuals who might well be in debt, unemployed, and/or homeless (Abadie 2010; Elliott 2014), and embedded in a social locale with particular standards and expectations. The discussion in this book frames the healthy volunteer as a subject in both social and institutional contexts because different political and institutional contexts may give participants different experiences. Petryna's (2005) work points to such variations in what she calls 'ethical variability' (p. 184) arguing that international codes of ethics governing human involvement in clinical drug trials fail to consider the local contexts and lived experiences and how these might shape people's experiences in clinical drug trials.

Incentives and Volunteering

Of interest in this book is the issue of incentives in phase I clinical drug trials and how they relate to healthy volunteering. The emergence of incentives for volunteers in clinical drug trials in the UK cannot be traced to a specific time, but allusions to the need to pay participants in research can be seen in the 1950s, when a government official talked of increasing payments to research participants at Porton Down. Some observers point to such changes in the early 1970s in response to the civil rights and anti-apartheid campaigns of the late 1960s, alongside public disquiet over the thalidomide disaster and the Tuskegee study (Bolton 2005; Abadie 2010). Bolton (2005) shows how in the early 1970s the use of the words ‘leisure’ and ‘holiday experience’ as part of the healthy volunteering emerged in advertisements and media coverage of health volunteering at CCRU and Porton Down, a centre for chemical and biological research in Wiltshire, UK.

During the same period, there were shifts in official discourse at Porton Down as officials started to portray participants in their experiments as volunteers. They were shown in advertisements as being relaxed, as though on holiday, amid entertainment facilities such as snooker tables. Advertisements also had the word ‘experiment’ removed from their titles to divert attention from any taint of negligence and abuse that was starting to appear in the media and in response to public disquiet over thalidomide and other such incidents (Goldby 1971; Hazelgrove 2002). As was common practice at the time, participants in these experiments were mainly army service personnel—people who are not normally asked for their consent, but who must obey commands from superiors. It seems questionable that their consent was ever sought or given.

Changes to funding following the economic downturn of the 1970s meant that by the early 1980s there was an increase in clinical drug trials as drug development was privatised (Mirowski and Horn 2005), resulting in further growth of the pharmaceutical industry. Developments in science, which led to a better understanding of the biology of the human body and its interactions with chemical agents, brought about further change. As clinical drug trials became established as standard practice in drug development, gradually they grew into a highly successful business leading to expansions of pharmaceutical companies such as Pfizer (Marks 2009) and contract research organisations (CROs), which conduct clinical drug trials on behalf of pharmaceutical companies. However, restrictions and regulation governing the recruitment of volunteers meant that readily available participants—for instance, prisoners—were no longer accessible (Abadie 2010). Instead, pharmaceutical companies had to depend on willing volunteers. In addition, the growing pressure to quickly develop commercially profitable drugs (Illich 1995) led to an increase in the demand for human volunteers on whom these IMPs had to be tested. This meant that human bodies became highly valuable resources for pharmaceutical companies, as scientists reconceptualised their objects of study "not as a people but as a population" which could be brokered as valuable research subjects in the commercial pharmaceutical context (Petryna 2005: 3).

It was during this period that incentives to encourage participation were introduced, which are still recognisable today. However, a specific discussion on incentives in healthy volunteering, as stated earlier, could be seen in experiments carried out at Porton Down, where it was argued that an incentive was needed to ensure wider involvement. Until 1955, service personnel who took part in studies at Porton Down were paid the sum of one shilling for risking their lives and health. But the Treasury was willing to increase the reward when the matter of extra pay was raised with the Treasury in a letter of October 17, 1955, by P.L. Burton of the War Office, in which he gave an overview of the history of the payment of 'servicemen volunteers' (Bolton 2005: 8). The rationale was that the tests were dangerous and unpleasant and that the payment of one shilling was not a sufficient incentive. Staff running the clinical trial unit asked for payment to be increased because of the dangerous and unpleasant nature of the work. Though payment was increased, it was discussed only in relation to service personnel at Porton Down, and there is no evidence that healthy volunteers involved in trials in other medical research were paid.

Currently, incentivising healthy volunteers is standard practice. In the UK payments to volunteers range from a few hundred pounds to about £3500 for a few days' stay in a trials unit and sometimes with 1 or 2 'outpatient' visits. To recruit, retain, and sustain an available pool of volunteers, CROs employ various media such as newspaper and website advertisements. The CROs call for interested individuals to register their interest, after which they are sent regular information as to when screening for trial commences. For example, an advertisement for healthy volunteers on Quintiles websites has in big bold letters with a picture of a supposed volunteer stating:

> Become one of our clinical trial volunteers - Simon participated in a trial to contribute to medical research. Do something rewarding. Our Clinical drug trials help everyone who has, or may someday have, a particular illness or condition by serving as a testing group for potentially helpful treatments. Clinical trial volunteers are key to the success of this research. So become a Quintiles research volunteer, and enjoy the rewards. (www.quintilesclinicaltrials.co.uk)

In this advert, note how altruism is invoked:asking volunteers to come forward to contribute to the development of medical research, which benefits the wider population. In this case, volunteering is framed as moral and a social good. Attention should also be paid to the emphasis on the supposed significance of volunteers to the research process by stating that 'volunteers are key to the success of the research. Such advertisements are common in some open calls for volunteers to register their interest in participation. Another advertisement from londontrial.com shows a call for volunteers both to a specific trial with financial rewards of £1500 for one trial and another for £2100. At the bottom of this page are two sections in bold letters highlighted in yellow with the following captions:

> Want to be a volunteer for a clinical trial and get paid?
>
> Paid Volunteering: it only takes a minute to register your interest to be a paid volunteer.

Of interest, this specific call to enrol in clinical drug trials emphasises the personal benefits healthy volunteers will obtain in the form of a financial rewards. Remarkably, calls for volunteers often focus on the morals of taking part, while at the same time shifting focus to portraying taking part in clinical drug trials as a comfortable and relaxed experience, akin to a holiday. In summary, the advertisements invoke firstly the rewards on offer to volunteers, and then turn to altruism in terms of the benefits to society in general; they make no reference to the risks associated with taking part in clinical drug trials.

Global Commercial and Political Context of Clinical Drug Trials

The use of incentives and shifts in the use of healthy participants in clinical drug trials should be seen in a global context. The evolution of the pharmaceutical industry as a profitable, successful business since the 1970s, has led to an increase in the demand for human subjects to take part in clinical drug trials. This demand has extended beyond national boundaries, with many clinical drug trials now moving offshore to poor and developing economies. As anthropologist Petryna (2005: 2) observes, clinical drug trials are migrating 'globally to so-called non-traditional research countries experiencing demographic change associated with declining health resources but having little or no share in the global pharmaceutical market'. Therefore, volunteering as a concept and in clinical trial contexts should be seen in this broader socioeconomic and political context.

Estimates suggest that by 2001 about 10,000 clinical drug trials had taken place worldwide (Petryna 2005: 2). By December 2015, about 202,378 clinical drug trials were taking place worldwide (U.S. National Institutes of Health), but this refers only to those registered with a clinical drug trials portal. This significant increase in the numbers of clinical drug trials conducted offshore is thought to be a result of the growing number of trials taking place every year, making volunteer numbers insufficient in the West. Additionally, the need to meet regulatory requirements has contributed to this increase; for example, in the US, where large numbers of participants are required before a drug is given marketing authorisation. On the other hand, calls by the International Conference on Harmonisation (ICH) for the creation of international regulations aided the growth of offshoring as the ICH allowed for the transfer of clinical data from international studies to the U.S. FDA for approval of new drugs (Petryna 2005). Recently the UK government has tried to bring about collaboration between pharmaceutical companies and the National Health Service (NHS) in later-phase trials, not only for the benefit of science but also with the stated aim to "improve" care within the NHS, clearly raising ethical (and sociological) concerns about the tensions between research and healthcare (Will 2011). The later-phase trials that are the subject of the proposed collaboration are often seen as part of the improvement of care in pioneering research and as a part of care for patients with conditions for whom existing treatments may not have worked. Early phase trials are not part of this collaboration; nonetheless, most of them are still conducted in the UK.

Furthermore, the global offshoring of clinical drug trials is influenced by the complex needs and healthcare situations in emerging economies. Reduced government funding for research and healthcare in these countries leaves local scientists and lay people open to taking part in these trials in the name of advancing science or having access to healthcare (Rajan 2006). Thus, scientists in these countries actively seek to establish contacts with CROs, hoping to host clinical drug trials (Petryna 2005). However, despite the growth in offshoring, the pharmaceutical industry is still very strong in the UK. According to the Office of National Statistics (ONS), the pharmaceutical industry contributes about three times the size of the textile and clothing industry combined to the UK economy (ONS 2014; Towse 1996).

Regarding the size of the pharmaceutical industry, as of January 2015 the Association of British Pharmaceutical Industry (ABPI), an influential organisation that lobbies the government and the EU on behalf of its members, had approximately 51 pharmaceutical companies and CROs registered as members (ABPI 2012). This number does not reflect the total number of companies operating in the UK, as membership of the ABPI is not mandatory. Furthermore, some of the larger pharmaceutical companies conduct some phase I trials on their own while some—especially small and upcoming pharmaceutical companies—contract out such drug trials to CROs to cut costs.

To illustrate the extent of the UK clinical drug trials industry, between 2005 and 2014 the Medicines and Healthcare products Regulatory Agency (MHRA), the UK's regulatory authorised body, received 10,411 applications for clinical drug trials. Of these, 2369 were phase I clinical drug trials. Of these phase I applications, 2241 were commercial applications, while 128 were non-commercial applications (MHRA 2014). Regarding CROs registered to conduct phase I trials in the UK, by November 2014, there were about 15 clinical drug trials units accredited as part of the MHRA phase I accreditation scheme aimed at licensing CROs to conduct phase I clinical drug trials. Under this scheme, which developed following the Northwick Park incident, CROs are only permitted to conduct a phase I clinical drug trials if they meet certain set criteria. Among the criteria is the need to have a principal investigator who has a qualification in conducting phase I clinical drug trials (MHRA 2014). All this illustrates the size of the clinical drug trials industry in the UK today. Additionally, this shows how CROs have to compete to attract and retain volunteers for their growing businesses.

CROs specialise in locating research sites, recruiting participants (as illustrated in an earlier section), and sometimes drafting the design and analysis of the study. The clients of CROs are pharmaceutical companies, who contract with them because they are seen as efficient, quick, and cheaper than the traditional academic institutions that used to carry out these functions (Petryna 2005). The role of biotechnology or pharmaceutical companies is to sponsor the clinical drug trials, while the CROs organise the trials in multiple centres, increasingly on a global scale. For far less invasive or less risky clinical drug trials, universities and other publicly funded institutions are used. However, although universities and other publicly funded laboratories continue to carry out low-risk studies and to play a major role in the development of drugs (identifying potential lead molecules, for example), the work required for the licensing of potentially good molecules tends to be given to CROs.

Consequently, the biomedical and experimental rationales for clinical drug trials have become interwoven with the market potential that these companies hope for, together with the risks inherent in the drug development process (Abraham 1997; Rajan 2005). This situation has fostered a collaborative relationship between corporations and universities. Though universities are key in identifying lead molecules, there are times when corporations have funded studies in universities, blurring the private versus public research divide (Petryna 2009). However, although studies in academic settings are usually deemed low-risk, they are not always free of controversy. In July 2002 a healthy volunteer died in the US after taking part in a study aimed at investigating the reflex that protects the lungs of healthy people against asthma attacks. She was required to inhale hexamenthonium, a substance once used to treat high blood pressure; afterwards she developed a cough, her condition worsened, and she died (Savulescu and Spriggs 2002). This example highlights the complexity in risk considerations associated with phase I trials. What might be deemed low risk and fit for 'relaxed' regulation might in fact be as risky as so-called high-risk studies.

The Demographics of Healthy Volunteers

Studies on healthy volunteering today allude to the phenomenon that poor populations, especially in developing countries, are tested with drugs, which, once approved, are sold to wealthy populations in the West (Shah 2006). In the absence of clear demographics, it is difficult to ascertain to what extent the poor are over-represented in clinical drug trials, and specifically in phase I clinical drug trials. Bioethicists Lurie, Wolfe, and Angell analyse later-phase trials in Asia and sub-Saharan Africa for the prevention of mother-to-child transmission of HIV, in which drugs were tested unethically on humans by researchers keen to obtain quick results (Lurie and Wolfe 2012; Angell 1997). Anthropologist Petryna (2009) considers the conduct of trials in Brazil and Eastern Europe on populations that are desperate to access healthcare.

While the issues that this literature raises are important, most of the focus has been on later-phase trials in resource-poor settings. There has been no sociological discussion on early-phase trials, whether or not they take place in poor countries, and how they are carried out. Within sociology, there have not been many quantitative studies that give demographic profiles of healthy volunteers (Tishler and Bartholomew 2002, 2003). As a result, there are no clear data showing the demographics of participants in the UK. A very illuminating recent study by physicians in Boston, Devine et al. (2013), note a tendency among healthy volunteers to use deception to gain admission into clinical drug trials. The study found a slight gender difference in healthy volunteering (male 57%; female 42%). With regard to income, 36% had a household income of $15,000 or less; 21% had household incomes ranging between $15,000 and $30,000. A further 30% had household incomes between $30,000 and $60,000. Eleven percent had household incomes ranging between $60,000 and $105,000. Interestingly, only one participant had come from a household income greater than $120,000. It is not clear whether this was the participant's income or the whole household's. The study also showed that participants in clinical drug trials in Boston are likely to have college-level education (UK equivalent of A levels and/or GCSE) or lower (62%), with the rest having completed some form of higher education qualification. Eighteen percent of the participants had undergraduate qualifications. Concerning employment, the study suggested that the 61% were not employed, disabled, or retired. The rest were in part-time work (8%) and about 11% in full-time work (Devine et al. 2013).

Devine et al.'s study findings contrast with most qualitative and quantitative social science research in the US. Fisher alone and with others, Tishler and Bartholomae (2002), Abadie (2010), Elliot (2008, 2014) alone and with others, argue that in the US, healthy volunteers are mostly disaffected ethnic minorities mostly with history of unemployment and are repeat volunteers. Precisely, recent studies by Fisher (2015) and Fisher and Monohan (2015) found that most participants in clinical drug trials were mostly men (73.6%) and were from ethnic minority backgrounds accounting for over 70% of the participants. Of all participants, about 80% were repeat volunteers. Most significantly, their study highlights that about 20% of participants were participating in phase I drug trials for the first time. This is important as it shows that healthy volunteering is not just attractive to repeat participants, but continues to attract new participants as well. Concerning employment, their study suggests about 17% of the participants were in full-time employment; the unemployed made up about 32% of the sample, with the rest being in part time employment. Elliot (2008) also points to this fact, arguing that some of the participants are not only economically disadvantaged, but also disenfranchised, such as the homeless and those with immigration issues. While Abadie's work in Philadelphia found that due to a lack of reasonably well-paid jobs and permanent employment among some social groups, healthy volunteering for some groups has become a profession. The aforementioned details illustrate how in the US context, healthy volunteering is clearly linked to disadvantage and economic or social precarity. Further afield in New Zealand, Tolich's (2010) research on healthy volunteers found that participants in phase I clinical drug trials there were mostly students looking for extra cash. However, it is not clear what the demographic characteristics of healthy volunteers in the UK are, and whether healthy volunteering in the UK would be the preserve of disadvantaged populations, as is the case in the US.

What these details invoke is a picture of healthy volunteers as generally those from low-income and financially vulnerable backgrounds. However, it should be noted that this picture may be true only of the US, and that in some other contexts, (e.g., the UK), healthy volunteers may well include people from different economic backgrounds.

Summary

To date there has been no research in the UK to explore only healthy volunteering; most research has focused on patient groups enrolled in trials (Featherstone 2003; Featherstone and Donovan 2002, 2003). While some studies have included aspects of healthy volunteering in their research (Corrigan 2003; Corrigan and Tutton 2006), which is encouraging, healthy volunteer involvement has often been conflated with patient participation in clinical drug trials. Problematically, this suggests that the needs and concerns of the two groups are the same, or even that ethical considerations are the same, when in fact they are different.

The subject in these chapters is the first sociological analysis of healthy volunteer experiences in the UK and the first to compare professional and lay views, experiences, and conceptions of risk in commercial phase I clinical drug trials. With increasing numbers of clinical drug trials taking place every year and a growing demand for human subjects, healthy volunteering has become common among sections of the British population, becoming what Schutz (1970: 139) called the social 'world of routine activities'. Healthy volunteering has become normalised in daily life. Investigating healthy volunteering in this context reveals the hidden social, political, and commercial contexts in which people engage with risk, and the problems resulting from medical technological innovations and increased commodification of the body. To that end, there is need to critically unpack the term 'volunteering', to reveal its complexity, and to show how, when uncritically used, the terms 'volunteer' and 'consent' can be harnessed as tools to exploit marginalised groups.

The following chapters document the dynamic and complex intersections of corporate and governance interests, and individual actions, to demonstrate how common conceptions of terms such as 'volunteer' and 'consent' in clinical drug trial settings raise questions about individual actions and to describe researcher and state responsibility to the volunteers. In Chap. 2, a discussion on risk and rationality is presented, arguing that the principles of bioethics of voluntary involvement and rational consent are compromised by the payments to participants in clinical trials. In Chap. 3, Alfred Schutz is my companion: I discuss the need for a phenomenological approach rather than one based on rationality and choice, in order to understanding healthy volunteer involvement in clinical drug trials. Chapter 4 Who Takes Part in Clinical Drug Trials? explores the demographics of healthy volunteers in the UK to illustrate differences in healthy volunteering between the US and the UK. Chapter 5, Context is Everything: The Reality of Becoming a Human Guinea Pig, discusses motivations for healthy volunteer involvement and argues that understanding why people choose to become guinea pigs requires appreciation of their individual circumstances. In Chap. 6, Economic Exchanges? Healthy Volunteering as a Form of Labour, Cooper and Waldby accompany me to problematize the role of payments in clinical drug trials to subjects who have no health benefit to gain from their involvement in such drug trials. I argue that emphasising voluntarism and rational consent while offering participants alluring financial rewards raises questions about the inviolability of ethical principles of avoiding use of force or coercion to research participants. To that end, healthy volunteering is located as form of labour. In Chap. 7, Volunteering for Free is Dead, Long Live Reciprocity? Revisiting the Gift Relationship, I reprise the discussion on voluntarism, consent, and rewards in clinical drug trials. The chapter questions long-standing views on altruism and giving as championed by Titmuss. Chapter 8, When Human Beings Become Guinea Pigs, closes the book. It is an invitation to reflect on role of healthy subjects in clinical drug trials and the conversations that must be had about their involvement. It ends with a call to action and what these actions could be.

Note

1. In 1937 a doctor in Tulsa, Oklahoma, USA, developed Elixir Sulfanilamide, as part of what was then a growing trend in the use of sulphonamides in Europe to treat common colds. However, Elixir Sulfanilamide itself, contained diethylene glycol, a highly toxic substance similar to ingredients found in anti-freeze and sold as an effective treatment for venereal diseases. People who consumed this drug become seriously ill and at least 73 people died. Following extensive media coverage, the U.S. FDA concluded that drugs should be tested before being put on the market.

References

Abadie, R. (2010). *The professional guinea pig: Big pharma and the risky world of human subjects*. London: Duke University Press.

ABPI. (2012). *Guidelines for phase 1 clinical drug trials* (2012 ed.). http://www.abpi.org.uk/our-work/library/guidelines/Pages/phase-1-trials-2012.aspx.

Abraham, J. (1997). The science and politics of medicines regulation. *Sociology of Health & Illness, 19*(19B), 153–182.

Angell, M. (1997). The ethics of clinical research in the third world. *New England Journal of Medicine, 337*, 847–848.

Armstrong, T. D., et al. (1999). Attitudes of African Americans toward participation in medical research. *Journal of Applied Social Psychology, 29*(3), 552–574.

Bartfai, T., & Lees, G. V. (2006). *Drug discovery: From bedside to Wall Street*. Cambridge: Academic Press.

Bolton, T. (2005). "Never volunteer for anything": The concept of the "volunteer" in human experimentation during the Cold War. *University of Sussex Journal of Contemporary History, 9*, 4–14.

Bourdieu, P. (2005). *The social structures of the economy*. Cambridge: Polity.

Carpenter, D. (2014). *Reputation and power: Organizational image and pharmaceutical regulation at the FDA: Organizational image and pharmaceutical regulation at the FDA*. Princeton, NJ: Princeton University Press.

Corrigan, O. (2003). Empty ethics: The problem with informed consent. *Sociology of Health & Illness, 25*(7), 768–792.

Corrigan, O., & Tutton, R. (2006). What's in a name? Subjects, volunteers, participants and activists in clinical research. *Clinical Ethics, 1*(2), 101–104.

Department of Work and Pensions. (2014). *Mandatory work activity provider guidance-incorporating universal credit UC guidance*. UK Government. https://www.gov.uk/government/uploads/system/uploads/attachment_data/file/420990/mandatory-work-activity-april-15.pdf.

Devine, E. G., et al. (2013). Concealment and fabrication by experienced research subjects. *Clinical Drug Trials, 10*(6), 935–948.

Edelblute, H. B., & Fisher, J. A. (2015). Using "clinical trial diaries" to track patterns of participation for serial healthy volunteers in US phase I studies. *Journal of Empirical Research on Human Research Ethics, 10*(1), 65–75.

Elliott, C. (2008). Guiea-pigging, Healthy human subjects for drug-safety trials are in demand. But is it a living?. *New Yorker* (New York, NY: 1925), 36–41.

Elliott, C. (2014, July 28). The best-selling, billion-dollar pills tested on homeless people: How the destitute and the mentally ill are being used as human lab rats. *Medium*, July 28. https://medium.com/matter/did-big-pharma-test-your-meds-on-homeless-people-a6d8d3fc7dfe.

Elliott, C., & Abadie, R. (2008). Exploiting a research underclass in phase 1 clinical drug trials. *New England Journal of Medicine, 358*(22), 2316–2317.

Epstein, S. (2004). Bodily differences and collective identities: The politics of gender and race in biomedical research in the United States. *Body & Society, 10*(2–3), 183–203.

Epstein, S. (2008). The rise of recruitmentology: Clinical research, racial knowledge, and the politics of inclusion and difference. *Social Studies of Science, 38*(5), 801–832.

Featherstone, K. (2003). The experience of trial participation [Editorial]. *The Journal of Rheumatology, 30*(4), 646–647.

Featherstone, K., & Donovan, J. L. (2002). "Why don't they just tell me straight, why allocate it?" The struggle to make sense of participating in a randomised controlled trial. *Social Science & Medicine, 55*(5), 709–719.

Featherstone, K., & Donovan, J. L. (2003). Random allocation or allocation at random? Patients' perspectives of participation in a randomised controlled trial. In M. Bury & J. Gabe (Eds.), *The sociology of health and illness: A reader*. London: Routledge.

Fisher, J. A. (2009). *Medical research for hire: The political economy of pharmaceutical clinical drug trials*. New Brunswick: Rutgers University Press.

Fisher, J. A. (2015). Feeding and bleeding: The institutional banalization of risk to healthy volunteers in phase I pharmaceutical clinical drug trials. *Science, Technology and Human Values, 40*(2), 199–226.
Fisher, J. A., & Kalbaugh, C. A. (2011). Challenging assumptions about minority participation in US clinical research. *American Journal of Public Health, 101*(12), 2217–2222.
Geissler, P. W. (2011). "Transport to where?": Reflections on the problem of value and time à propos an awkward practice in medical research. *Journal of Cultural Economy, 4*(1), 45–64.
Goldacre, B. (2012). *Bad pharma: How drug companies mislead doctors and harm patients.* London: Fourth Estate.
Goldby, S. (1971). Experiments at the Willowbrook State School. *The Lancet, 297*(7702), 749.
Guideline, ICH Harmonised Tripartite. (2009). *Nonclinical evaluation for anticancer pharmaceuticals S9.* International Conference on Harmonization.
Gupta, P., et al. (2012). Phase I clinical drug trials of anticancer drugs in healthy volunteers: Need for critical consideration. *Indian Journal of Pharmacology, 44*(4), 540.
Hallowell, N., et al. (2010). An investigation of patients' motivations for their participation in genetics-related research. *Journal of Medical Ethics, 36*(1), 37–45.
Harris, Y., et al. (1996). Why African Americans may not be participating in clinical drug trials. *Journal of the National Medical Association, 88*(10), 630.
Hazelgrove, J. (2002). The old faith and the new science: The Nuremberg code and human experimentation ethics in Britain, 1946–1973. *Social History of Medicine, 15*(1), 109–135.
Hedgecoe, A. (2013, October). A deviation from standard design? Clinical drug trials, research ethics committees and the regulatory co-construction of organizational deviance. *Social Studies of Science,44*(1), 59–81.
Illich, I. (1995). *Limits to medicine: Medical nemesis—The expropriation of health.* New York: Marion Boyars Publishers, Incorporated.
Kerr, D., et al. (Eds.). (2006). *Clinical drug trials explained: A guide to clinical drug trials in the NHS for healthcare professionals.* Oxford: Blackwell.
Kohli-Laven, N., et al. (2011). Cancer clinical drug trials in the era of genomic signatures: Biomedical innovation, clinical utility, and regulatory-scientific hybrids. *Social Studies of Science, 41*(4), 487–513.
Lemmens, T., & Elliott, C. (1999). Guinea pigs on the payroll: the ethics of paying research subjects. *Accountability in research, 7*(1), 3–20.
Lemmens, T., & Elliott, C. (2001). Justice for the professional guinea pig. *American journal of bioethics, 1*(2), 51–53.
Lurie, P., & Wolfe, S. M. (1997). Unethical trials of interventions to reduce perinatal transmission of the Human Immunodeficiency Virus in developing countries. *New England Journal of Medicine, 337*(12), 853–856.

Lurie, P., & Wolfe, S. M. (2012). Unethical trials of interventions to reduce perinatal transmission of the Human Immunodeficiency Virus in developing countries. *Arguing About Bioethics*, 479.

Marks, H. (2009). What does evidence do? Histories of therapeutic research. In C. Bonah (Ed.), *Harmonizing drugs. Standards in 20th-century pharmaceutical history*. Paris: Glyphe.

MHRA. (2014). *UK clinical trial authorisation assessment performance*. http://www.mhra.gov.uk/Howweregulate/Medicines/Licensingofmedicines/Clinicaltrials/UKclinicaltrialauthorisationassessmentperformance/index.htm.

Mirowski, P., & Van Horn, R. (2005). The contract research organization and the commercialization of scientific research. *Social Studies of Science, 35*(4), 503–548.

Monahan, T., & Fisher, J. A. (2015). "I'm Still a Hustler": Creative and entrepreneurial responses to precarity by participants in phase I clinical drug trials. *Economy and Society, 44*, 545–566.

Mwale, S. (2016). Same difference? From Northwick park in 2006 to Rennes in 2016. *Cost of Living Blog*. http://www.cost-ofliving.net/same-difference-from-northwick-park-in-2006-to-rennes-in-2016/.

Nelson, E. (2005). Liberty: One concept too many? *Political Theory, 33*, 58–78.

ONS (2014). What does the UK pharmaceutical industry look like today? Part of Index of Production. Release available at http://www.ons.gov.uk/ons/rel/iop/index-of-production/april-2014/sty-pharmaceuticals.html accessed 15 January 2015.

Pappworth, M. H. (1967). Experiments on man. *British Medical Journal, 3*(5565), 616.

Petryna, A. (2005). Ethical variability: Drug development and globalizing clinical drug trials. *American Ethnologist, 32*(2), 183–197.

Petryna, A. (2009). *When experiments travel: Clinical drug trials and the global search for human subjects*. Princeton: Princeton University Press.

Petryna, A., & Kleinman, A. (2006). The pharmaceutical nexus. In A. Petryna, A. Lakoff, & A. Kleinman (Eds.), *Global pharmaceuticals: Ethics, markets, practices*. Durham: Duke University Press.

Pocock, J. (2000). *Clinical drug trials: A practical approach*. Chichester: Wiley.

Rägo, L., & Santoso, B. (2008). Drug regulation: History, present and future. *Drug benefits and risks: International textbook of clinical pharmacology* (Rev. 2nd ed.). Available at: http://www.who.int/entity/medicines/technical_briefing/tbs/Drug_Regulation_Histoy_Present_Future.pdf.

Rajan, K. S. (2005). Subjects of speculation: Emergent life sciences and market logics in the United States and India. *American Anthropologist, 107*(1), 19–30.

Rajan, K. S. (2006). *Biocapital: The constitution of postgenomic life*. Durham: Duke University Press.

Rosner, D. (1996). Human guinea pigs: Medical experimentation before World War II. *JSTOR*. http://www.jstor.org/stable/30030721.

Savulescu, J., & Spriggs, M. (2002). The hexamethonium asthma study and the death of a normal volunteer in research. *Journal of Medical Ethics, 28*(1), 3–4.

Schutz, A. (1970). *Reflections on the problem of relevance* (R. M. Zaner, Trans.). New Haven: Yale University Press.

Scocozza, L. (1989). Ethics and medical science. On voluntary participation in biomedical experimentation. *Acta Sociologica, 32*(3), 283–293 (Taylor & Francis Ltd).

Shah, S. (2006). *The body hunters: Testing new drugs on the world's poorest patients*. New York: New Press.

Sondhi, G. (2013). *Gendering international student mobility: An Indian case study*. Available at: http://sro.sussex.ac.uk/46066/1/Sondhi,_Gunjan.pdf.

Stebbings, R., Poole, S., & Thorpe, R. (2009). Safety of biologics, lessons learnt from TGN1412. *Current Opinion in Biotechnology, 20*(6), 673–677.

Tolich, M. (2010). What if Institutional Research Boards (IRBs) treated healthy volunteers in clinical trials as their clients? *Australasian Medical Journal, 3*(12), 767–771. doi 10.4066/AMJ.2010.431

Tishler, C. L., & Bartholomae, S. (2002). The recruitment of normal healthy volunteers: A review of the literature on the use of financial incentives. *The Journal of Clinical Pharmacology, 42*(4), 365–375.

Tishler, C. L., & Bartholomae, S. (2003). Repeat participation among normal healthy research volunteers: Professional guinea pigs in clinical trials? *Perspectives in Biology and Medicine, 46*(4), 508–520.

Towse, A. (1996). The UK pharmaceutical market. *PharmacoEconomics, 10*(2), 14–25.

Washington, H. A. (2006). *Medical Apartheid: The dark history of medical experimentation on Black Americans from colonial times to the present*. New York: Doubleday.

Weber, M., Swindler, A., & Parsons, T. (1963). *The sociology of religion*. Boston, MA: Beacon Press.

Will, C. M. (2011). Mutual benefit, added value? *Journal of Cultural Economy, 4*(1), 11–26.

Wilson, J. (2000). Volunteering. *Annual Review of Sociology, 26*(1), 215–240.

Wilson, J., & Musick, M. (1999). The effects of volunteering on the volunteer. *Law and contemporary problems, 62*(4), 141–168.

Wuthnow, R. (1993). Altruism and sociological theory. *The Social Service Review, 67*(3), 344–357.

CHAPTER 2

Risk, Rewards, and Rational Consent in Healthy Volunteering

Abstract This chapter explores the limitations of the 'rational' and 'capable' perspective to understanding healthy volunteer involvement in clinical drug trials. The chapter considers sociological approaches to studying risk and rationality. It questions the uncritical ways in which rational choice theory within a liberal economic context has influenced conceptions of individuals in bioethics' principles about human involvement in clinical drug trials. In conclusion, I show the limitations of the common approaches to understanding healthy volunteer involvement in clinical drug trials.

Keywords Rationality · Bodies · Risk · Clinical drug trials · Value consent · Clinical labour

Sociology and Rationality

Rationality as a concept in everyday life has been of interest in sociology from its inception. In the 19th and early 20th centuries, Marx (1961) and Weber (1978) both looked at questions of motivation and rationality. Weber's approach focused on explanations for actions. Over time, this work has come to be interpreted as a focus on the verbal justifications or accounts given as reasons for their questioned conduct (Campbell 1996). The approach developed from what Campbell calls the uncritical reading of Wright Mills's definition of motive as 'anticipated situational consequences of questioned conduct' (Mills 1940, 970).

S. Mwale, *Healthy Volunteers in Commercial Clinical Drug Trials*,
DOI 10.1007/978-3-319-59214-5_2

This definition resulted in the rise of what came to be known as the 'vocabulary of motives tradition of inquiry' within sociology (Campbell 1996, 101), in which Wright Mills' definition was taken to refer to how motives are presented as explanations in defence of questioned conduct. But as Campbell argues, this view is contrary to both Weber's and Wright Mills' original understanding of motive as a concept. For Wright Mills, motives should not be seen as mere expressions of intentions and separate from actions; rather, the verbalisation of motive is itself an act just as much as the actions or behaviours in question are. Therefore, analysis of motive should consider more than just the words used in the assumption but should also include the context in which the account is given, as well as where the act in question takes place.

To that end, it is fair to say rationality as a concept is a highly contested subject in sociology. Rational choice theorists make several assumptions about individuals as actors (Becker 1993); simply put, these can be summarised as follows; firstly, individuals have preferences and these are reflected in their goals in life in general. These goals are beyond the theorists' moral, value, and validity judgment, rather, these are accepted as they are. Secondly, individuals are seen as averse to pain but having an affinity for pleasure. Therefore, individuals are considered to be motivated by the need to avoid pain, while maximising net benefits. They engage in a balancing of the costs against benefits. Furthermore, individuals are seen to be selfish in their pursuit of their preferences concerned only with their own benefits. Lastly, people are considered to be rational; by 'rational', they refer to individuals having a tendency to behave consistently in their pursuit of their goals, by weighing the gains against the costs, and always choosing an option that leads to maximum net benefit or minimum net cost. These very simplified points sum up what rational choice theorist call 'the logic of rational choice' (Becker 1993).

The limitations of this way of looking at people have been well-documented, including arguments that such a view does not consider actions that would otherwise be seen as nonrational. To that end, new approaches focusing on subjective rather than objective rationality have emerged (Horlick-Jones 2005). Despite these limitations, the rational choice theory is still very influential today. It is common in public health and bioethics, as we will discuss later, in the context of neoliberal economics to think of individuals as capable and rational in representing their interests. By neoliberal, I refer to aspects of the liberal traditions that stand against government intervention, in the form of regulation, in economic matters. In this way, individuals are seen as rational and capable of participating freely in self-regulating markets. State regulation is reduced to creating a milieu that fosters a free market or imposing protectionist policies to favour local industry and commerce. Neoliberal approaches are demonstrated in state policies of privatisation of public services, including aspects of research and deregulation (Massey 2013). As Fisher (2009) observes, neoliberalism also entails the state's transfer of its responsibilities to the individual citizen. All this is packaged and presented in the rhetoric of individual liberties, in which the state should not interfere with individual choices; rather, people should be allowed to participate on their own accord in the market, thereby providing for themselves. Overall, ideas of individuals as rational actors have become useful justifications for policy approaches in market economies.

It is not surprising therefore, that rationality and motivation have been subjects of interest in much sociological debates, precisely focusing on explanations for individual's action, in relation to issues ranging from motivations to the kinds of reasoning used by lay people when engaging with science and medicine. Lay reasoning has been well-documented in recent research, such as a study on health-seeking behaviours in smoking-cessation programmes (Bond et al. 2012) and immunisation. In such sociological studies, the focus has been on finding logic in lay reasoning. For example, Rogers and Pilgrim's (1995) study of public resistance to mass childhood immunisation considered how the public construct their own risk assessments. A study by Hobson-West (2003) explored the logic of public resistance against vaccinations in the UK and the implications of this resistance for public health. Hobson-West argues that rather than seeing public resistance to vaccinations as a misconception of risks, or that public decisions on risk are based on comparisons of individual risk, such conceptions of risk and resistance should instead be seen simply as a different way of comprehending health and disease as categories. A similar anthropological study by Poltorak et al. (2004) considers the contexts in which resistance to measles, mumps and rubella (MMR) vaccination takes place. Their research investigated parental choice in seeking to explain resistance to immunisation and draws attention to the wider social and personal issues that shape parents' views on immunisation. Similarly, Mishra and Graham (2012) explored attempts to prevent cervical cancer using vaccination against the human papilloma virus (HPV). The study focused on the representation of young women as autonomous rational actors in a campaign to reduce cervical cancer in

Canada. In sum, it has become important to explore how people make decisions. In this book, I explore people's motivations to become healthy volunteers and how they account for the attendant risks.

Sociological Conceptions of Risk

Closely linked to attempts to understand rationality has been the focus on lay or public understandings of risk. Risk is a highly contested concept within the social sciences. For centuries, society has attempted to define measure, identify, and predict risk. However, as a concept within social science, risk has become more topical in the recent past (Beck 1992). Risk as a concept relates to the probability of events happening and their potential effects in terms of losses or gains, mostly because of some activity or policy (MØldrup and Morgall 2001; Taylor-Gooby and Zinn 2006). There have been several sociological attempts to theorise risk and today debates about what constitutes risk have become symptomatic of what Giddens (2013) and Beck (1992) call'risk society'. However, others such as Green (2009) have challenged the usefulness of risk as a concept in sociological analysis of health issues. While this debate is important, it is beyond the scope of this book. However, knowledge of the value of risk in this sociological literature informed my analysis and was useful in conceptualising my lay participants' understanding and decision-making about the riskiness of their activities.

In this book, I discuss risk in relation to how it is mediated or defined by institutions, and from a lay individual's perspective. In relation to expert and institutional conceptions of risk, sociologists such as Wynne (1996) have explored and critiqued common institutional conceptions of risk in technical and analytical terms (Wynne 1996). This institutional conception of risk situates risk as purely a technical issue amenable to expert measurement and ranking using statistical models and thus can be mitigated against (Fiorino 1990). This emanates from institutions insuring against risk through insurance companies; in turn, deriving from fears of individuals suing. This leads to highly risk-averse policies and practices in institutions imposed by insurance companies, for whom a 1% chance of an adverse event will mean large numbers of claims taken across their whole portfolio. Within this context, risk decisions are thought to be the domain of experts who mediate and define risk for the public. In my discussion, this is linked to the institutional approaches to managing risks and uncertainty (Brown and Calnan 2010) associated with adverse drug reactions in the drug-development process. It is also looked at in terms of the roles played by the MHRA's clinical drug trials assessment and licensing team who evaluate the safety of the chemical compounds in IMP formulations to ascertain drug safety and RECs. Broadly, within this framework, the experts' role is to define, assess, and certify risks as tolerable, and mitigate against risk, while lay individuals are seen as rational and capable of making informed decision if provided with expert information. Hillman (1993) alone and with others, has explored how institutional conceptions of risks of cycling on inner-city roads influences public perceptions of the risks associated with cycling. They argue that the mistaken view that cycling is riskier than travel by car has led to fewer people taking to cycling due to the perceived risk of accidents associated with cycling. This is of significance as it illustrates how institutions and experts play a role in shaping lay views and responses to risk. Horlick-Jones (2004) looked at the emergence of new forms of expertise on risk and how experts are challenged by the changing characteristics of risks itself. Wynne (1996) and Taylor-Gooby and Zinn (2006) among others in their work have explored differences between institutional and lay conceptions of risk. This difference in views means that lay responses to risks are often at odds with expert advice and prescriptions. Walls et al. (2004) explored how presence or lack of what he calls 'critical trust' in the relationship between the lay public and institutions that define and mediate risk influences public responses and actions to risk. Brown and Calnan (2010) have looked at the role of trust between lay individuals and institutions in understanding lay responses to risk. This is discussed to some detail later in this chapter. In short, expert definitions and communications of risk tend to negate people's lived experiences and how these shape people's understanding and engagement with risk.

There has been extensive research on risk and lay individual action in sociology among others relating to lay understandings of health and risk. For instance, taking a broad approach, Horlick-Jones's (2005) paper on logics of risk examines how discussion of public or individual rationality and irrationality often assumes a canonical conception of reason, which posits individuals as purely rational and calculative in their actions (Scott 2000). However, as Horlick-Jones argues, in practice lay public's everyday engagement with and conception of risk is contingent on the context, and thus adopts a more practical reasoning approach than a canonical approach. Of particular relevance to my argument, on the significance of context in understanding the interaction between health and risk is Bloor's (1995) study of HIV and AIDS transmission. In his work, Bloor explores gay male prostitutes' conception of risk. The study demonstrates how people's engagement with risk is contingent on the contextual power relationships in social interactions. Tulloch and Lupton (2003), among others, look at individual responses to risk in diverse social situations. Peretti-Watel and Moatti (2006) and Peretti-Watel et al. (2007) have explored conceptions of risky behaviours in health promotion settings. Their findings suggest that labelling people who engage in "risky" behaviours as delinquents brings about pressure to conform to social norms. This may make people deny the risky label or even the fact that their actions are actually risky, resulting in an escalation of the risky behaviour. Of interest in Peretti-watel et al. (2007) findings is how repeated engagement with risk results in individuals conceiving of risk as diminishing and in some cases as absent.

In this book, I approach risk by building on Lyng's (2005) concept of edgework, in which he considers risk-taking as related to the 'consequences of political, economic and scientific progress' and their impact on 'health and wellbeing' (Lyng 2009, 107), resulting in public willingness to engage with risk and the advent of positive views of risk-taking behaviours. According to Lyng, this has stemmed from wide-ranging 'neoliberal' policies and political initiatives, specifically in Western societies, which have shifted responsibility for welfare such as health and employment from the state to the individual. In drawing on Lyng's conception of risk, I am focusing on healthy volunteering in clinical drug trials not as a leisure activity but as a form of voluntary risk-taking in which the 'choice' to engage with risk is defined, as in high-risk sports, by class, race, cultural, socioeconomic, and sociopolitical factors.

So far, the studies discussed in this section all have a common theme: understanding individual rationality. Most emphasise the significance of context in understanding risk. In general, with regard to clinical drug trials, society and professionals recognise that people grapple with issues around risk in clinical drug trials and that these are often thought to be resolved by the application of procedures informed by bioethics.

Bioethics and the Logic of Human Involvement in Clinical Drug Trials

The topic under discussion in this book lies at the intersection between healthy volunteering and institutional contexts. While the sociological research I discussed earlier focuses on the rationality of the lay public in relation to risk, the application of the canonical conceptions of rationality has not been limited to economics and psychology (Horlick-Jones 2005). Rather, the influence of established conceptions of individual action can also be seen in disciplines such as bioethics. Discussions regarding human involvement in medical research usually have been considered as the domain of medical ethics or bioethics (Evans 2000).

Bioethics is distinguished from medical ethics in that it is broadly concerned with attending to a variety of new developments in biological sciences. These include ethical concerns emanating from experiments and human involvement in clinical drug trials. Medical ethics, on the other hand, is an older discipline dealing with ethical concerns arising from the practice of medicine (Bosk 1999; Hedgecoe 2004). My discussion focuses on bioethics and specifically on the principlist approach (Evans 2000) that guides the practice of medical and pharmaceutical research. Following the ban of forced use of human subjects in medical research at Nuremberg (Scocozza 1989), the guidelines were established with emphasis on voluntary involvement in clinical drug trials. My aim here is not to give a historical account of the Nuremberg code, or to imply that this was the only important event in the history of ethics and medical experimentation. There have been many incidents over the years pertaining to clinical drug trials, illustrated by the Tuskegee (Harris et al. 1996) and thalidomide (Hazelgrove 2002) disasters (outlined in Chap. 1). I raise the Nuremberg code because it made incidents in medical research visible, and it is also a useful reference point for starting to change guidelines and attitudes about human involvement.

Since its inception, the Nuremberg Code has undergone several revisions and has evolved into fundamental guiding principles for human involvement in clinical drug trials internationally. The involvement of WHO in promoting these principles and the signing by many countries of these international codes of practice of medical research are indications of how bioethics has become part of clinical trial organisation and regulation, and is now woven into codes of practice at national and institutional levels in many countries, including the UK (what I call 'institutionalised ethics'). Bioethics has become institutionalised in the regulatory system as a tool regulating and legitimising clinical drug trials and is the hub on which the moral practice of pharmaceutical research is based. These principles have been influential in shaping policy debates about human involvement in medical research (Evans 2000; Dingwall 2008). Today debates about safety, consent, and payment of volunteers are imbued with this traditional bioethical discourse, including a commitment to avoid harming participants and, in a larger sense, achieving good. This discussion focuses on the dominant principles-based approach of bioethics, and how they have become socially and institutionally established as a moral platform and linked to ideas of formal rationality (Evans 2000). Here differences should be noted between bioethics as practice and bioethics as a discipline. As a discipline, bioethics is concerned with other principles, such as avoiding harm and duty of care, in addition to autonomy and rational consent. These other principles are equally relevant because they relate to questions about the boundaries between care and medical research in patient involvement in clinical drug trials (Will 2011), which may easily become blurred as medical professionals assume the roles of both researcher and healthcare professional. Here, I consider two principles of bioethics: rational consent or autonomy and voluntarism.

Rational Consent and Autonomy

One of the major tenets of biomedical ethics is rational consent. This principle assumes that to ensure and protect participants' interests in medical or any other research, they should be offered full information (Scocoza 1989; Hoeyer 2009) upon which to base their decision to take part. Within this framework, the provision of full information is considered to resolve most ethical issues as information provision is seen as an enabler for participants to make free and rational decisions about their involvement. Thus, rational consent is seen as counter to tyrannical and paternalistic medical research practices (Weindling 2001; Dingwall 2008). This model of the autonomous individual is consistent with Giddens's (1991) conceptualisation of a rational, free-acting, and calculative individual, and is attractive to governmental regulatory cultures, particularly in Western neoliberal society with its focus on the autonomous individual and his or her rights.

Autonomy is taken to mean the ability to act freely without restriction or coercion (Beauchamp and Childress 2001). With regard to clinical drug trials, it is often assumed that people take part out of a rational, informed choice. However, using autonomy in such a way negates the social circumstances and the wider social and political contexts in which informed decisions are made. This is because the process of consent takes place within contexts of power and against a backdrop of cultural norms that shape the way freedom and choice are experienced by individuals. In addition, the interactions in which 'consent' is given 'involves continual negotiation of power that is contingent upon the context' (Lupton 2000, 104) in which the interaction takes place. But one may also draw from Milgram's (1963) experiments on how those in authority may influence people's reactions to risk or obedience to requests, thus compromising the consent process. This further illustrates how power imbalances in relationships may affect what people take on trust. Thus people are likely to be less critical and more ready to believe doctors or other medical personnel, who may be seen as rational and altruistic and often are held in high esteem.

Voluntarism

Another key principle of bioethics, and closely linked to the principle of rational consent, is the view that anyone involved in clinical drug trials or medical research should voluntarily take part. As a principle in bioethics, voluntarism dictates that human subjects are expected to consent willingly, coming forward on their own accord and not forced or deceived into taking part. The aim of introducing voluntarism in the Nuremberg code was to restore agency and protect human dignity in medical research. I must emphasise that 'coercion' here refers to making people participate in clinical drug trials as research subjects using force or deception, by taking advantage of people's vulnerable circumstances such as prisoners and slaves. However, coercion was also drawn from economic conceptions of individuals as capable of freely acting and rational action (Becker 1963). To volunteer, therefore, meant people could choose to take part in clinical drug trials without any force, coercion, or deceit. In 1964, the Helsinki Declaration revised the Nuremberg Code to draw specific attention to vulnerable people such as patients, children, and those considered mentally incapable of making their own decisions; these groups would require special protection in law. People who did not fit these criteria were (and are still) assumed capable of making rational decisions and representing their own interests.

Consequently, this shift to voluntarism destabilised what were then established sources of human subjects for research: vulnerable and captive populations such as prisoners and service personnel. However, it is argued that forceful and deceitful use of prisoners for research in the UK has never been a problem historically. Whether this is true is a matter open to debate. Nonetheless, these groups were now no longer readily available for use in medical research. Subsequently, researchers had to start thinking of new ways of recruiting participants while adhering to the new legislation and requirements regarding recruitment of volunteer human subjects. However, it appears that regulators focused too much on a definition of coercion that involved forcefully and deceitfully recruiting people for medical research. They did not consider the subtler ways in which coercion might work (O'Neill 2003; Moser et al. 2004), particularly the introduction of payments. In other words, paying volunteers was not considered to be seen as a kind of coercion for people who needed money.

A Sociological Critique of the Two Principles of Bioethics

Payments and Voluntarism

As the business of clinical drug trials grew from the 1970s onwards, human research subjects became a scarce resource. It was during this period that incentives to volunteers were introduced as part of the commercialisation and privatisation of medical research. For instance, by April 1984, there was such a strong commercial interest in setting up clinical trial units that the UK government commissioned a working party to consider issues such as the licensing of clinical trial units, volunteer health and safety, and the impact of payments to volunteers for medical research. The measure came in response to requests by the Medicines Commission, which had become concerned about the increase in clinical drug trials requiring healthy volunteers both in the private sector and in the NHS (Royal College of Physicians 1986). The growth in commercial clinical trial units resulted in a market-oriented approach; healthy volunteers became commodities who could be 'bought' on the market. Human subjects in medical research came to be viewed as volunteers and capable of rational consent, meaning that from the 1970s onwards, healthy volunteers in particular started to be seen as capable of pursuing and protecting their interests, just as though they were making transactions in a market economy. While it must be acknowledged that in deciding whether to take part in clinical drug trials, subjects are involved in weighing risks against gains, most social scientists (Corrigan 2003; Fisher 2007) argue that if potential participants are promised large sums as rewards for their involvement, it problematises the entire notion of both rational consent and volunteering itself.

This is because payments are at odds with the principle of noncoercive involvement as they raise the possibility that participants being exploited as volunteers are likely to be from economically disadvantaged backgrounds (Schonfeld et al. 2007). This has been found to be true in a variety of studies (Fisher 2015; Petryna 2009; Abadie 2010). All these studies highlight how structural inequalities—among volunteers and professionalsand citizens of different countries—and payments to research participants in developing countries undermine the idea of autonomy in consent and raise ethical dilemmas of potential coercion (Fisher 2015; Geissler 2011) .

Currently, paying volunteers for involvement in phase 1 clinical drug trials is common practice, though incentives are also common in later-phase studies as well. This illustrates the complexity of payments to volunteers in clinical drug trials. Geissler (2011) looks at how volunteers in an HIV and AIDS vaccine clinical trial in Kenya were offered a bar of soap as an incentive and had their transport costs reimbursed. However, most of the volunteers are thought to have walked to the clinics and the transport refund came to more than the daily cost of living, thus being a kind of payment for participation in the trials. The researchers were aware of the anomaly, yet the official line was that participants were not being paid.

Corrigan's work examines whether participants in clinical drug trials in the UK understand the rational consent process. Petryna focuses on how late-phase clinical drug trials are being increasingly offshored to developing countries in South America, Eastern Europe, Asia, and Africa, in search of populations thought to be less medicated than those in the West (and therefore more likely to volunteer because of their need for medication), economically straitened, and living in countries where costs of clinical drug trials are low and regulation is not as strict as in the West.

Researchers and governments in these countries see pharmaceutical studies as sources of research funding and employment. However, most participants in these trials are poor people who cannot afford healthcare. Anthropological studies by Petryna (2009), Glickman et al. (2009), and Rajan (2006), among others, on the global political economy of pharmaceutical research highlight how the increasing commercialisation and outsourcing of clinical drug trials abroad raise the risk that research will rely unduly—and unjustly—on economically vulnerable populations. These studies challenge Beck's argument that risks in the 'risk society' have been democratised. Schonfeld et al. (2007) argue that the risks in clinical drug trials are borne disproportionately by vulnerable social groups who volunteer for the reward on offer.

This makes the issue of monetary inducement ethically relevant in clinical drug trials. It draws attention to the subtleties of coercion. The difficulty with over-emphasising rationality is that it negates how people with low incomes and those in debt (Weinstein 2001) and/or unemployed see the sums offered for participation in clinical drug trials as life-changing. Of course, for others such sums may offer relatively little inducement. Nor does it account for the ways in which interactions between professionals and the public are based on interdependencies and reciprocities. For instance, studies in the US have found that to gain admission to as many paid clinical drug trials as possible, healthy volunteers were likely to use deception such as denying being on any treatment, using recreational drugs, or involvement in other trials (Bentley and Thacker 2004; Devine et al. 2013). Such practices undermine clinical drug trials as a system of drug development. In addition, this demonstrates how incentives in clinical drug trials are methodologically unsound and inefficient, and undermine the principles of bioethics.

Another observation of note is that at both national and international levels, regulation has been vague if not silent about how payments should be calculated (Lemmens and Elliott 1999). Similarly, there are no clear definitions of how long a healthy volunteer can stay between clinical trial involvements. This silence is symptomatic of the assumption of capability on the part of healthy volunteers to represent their own interests and make rational decisions and government attempts to avoid 'interfering' with the market.

Healthy Volunteering: An Economic Exchange and a Form of Labour

In view of the preceding discussion, within medical research today, human involvement may be conceptualised as an economic exchange: healthy individuals are used to test new drugs in exchange for the money offered by research companies (Elliott 2014; Abadie 2010). This exchange can be traced back to mediaeval times. As illustrated in Chap. 1, until recently the captive populations were used as subjects for such trials because it enabled them to receive healthcare and in some cases test the remedies of their masters (Washington 2006; Weinstein 2001). I am aware of arguments that considering human involvement in clinical trial as an economic exchange undermines the ideal of voluntarism and its significance in social relations (Geisler 2011). However, important as the term 'volunteer' might be, it would be naïve to ignore how it is used discursively in clinical drug trials to obscure inequalities and the creation of value in clinical drug trials. In Marxist political economic terms, volunteers can be thought of as a type of worker who contributes to the creation of commodities—namely—medicines, which have a market value. 'Exploitation' occurs if they are paid less than the portion of value that they create. Anthropologists Petryna (2005, 2009) and Rajan (2006), and sociologists Cooper and Waldby (2002) illustrate how recent biotechnological developments have transformed the bodies of human research subjects and all their constituent parts into valuable material. Blood serves as the basis for immortalised cell lines and is an important commodity in pharmaceutical research. Sperm, embryos, and other body parts such as kidneys have acquired commercial value both to pharmaceutical companies and to the public, especially financially disadvantaged people.

The demand for healthy volunteers in medical research has led pharmaceutical companies to search locally and globally for cheap and accessible subjects. Petryna draws attention to how the application of ethics seems to vary across international boundaries, specifically among populations of different economic status; such variability obscures who governs the conduct of clinical drug trials and who is responsible for protecting the rights of clinical trial participants. Petryna's notion of ethical variability is significant in in this discussion as it points to the need for an interrogation of regulatory frameworks and the interpretation of ethical guidelines. Moreover, professionals with easy access to bodies realise they possess a capital resource (Petryna 2009), despite the risk of harm that their products and trials hold for humans. The difficulties of recruitment and efficient running of trials have provided a growing market for CROs, which recruit subjects and carry out research on behalf of big pharmaceutical companies, and there is increasing competition for research subjects.

Keeping with the same theme Cooper and Waldby (2002) observe that in post-Fordist political economies, there has been a shift from mass production to service economies and knowledge production. Cooper and Waldby argue that the response of post-industrial economies to emerging economies has been to focus not on mass production but on biotechnological and ontological innovations that would surpass the achievements of the post-industrialisation era. The accompanying policy discourse has focused on the unrealised potentials of biofuels, genome projects, and efforts to harness them for the growth of their economies,with little focus on how ideas move from the lab to products via experiments and clinical drug trials on human subjects. Consequently, the organisation of labour has resulted in flexible work being introduced, the weakening of organised forms of labour replaced by individual contracts in which individuals rather than employers are responsible for the risks and safety at work.

Turning this analytical framework to human involvement in medical research, Cooper and Waldby (2002) illustrate what they call 'clinical labour' in which human bodies are exploited to create value. Here the bodies of some groups have become not only resources, but also a site for clinical research. Of significance is how the body is used in the fertility industry in relation to surrogacy in developing economies such as India, and of course healthy volunteers in clinical drug trials. In this context, therefore, human subjects are seen as individual contractors who are capable of rational action. Since the 1950s, medical technological innovations have increased transfers of body parts in complex operations to save lives or pursue goals such as parenthood. While most of these parts can be harvested from cadavers, organs and tissues such as kidneys and bone marrow from living persons today are common candidates for transfer. It is not only institutions that see the body as a resource; individuals, too, see the potential of their bodies to generate income. Medical actors on both sides of the equation are trying to make the most of this resource. There has recently been a growing supply of surrogate mothers and egg and sperm donations among poor communities in parts of India (Roberts and Scheper-Hughes 2011). Today the pharmaceutical industry demands increasing numbers of research participants and the search for volunteers has gone beyond national boundaries.

Healthy Volunteering as 'Passive Labour'

The growth in CROs and the global scramble for healthy subjects for clinical drug trials is an illustration of the value that human subjects in research contribute to the bio-economy. I add here that these new forms of value creation challenge common conceptions of 'normal work' and definitions of acceptable means of 'making a living'. In my view, it is through the process of 'passive labour' that value is produced beyond the limits of socially acceptable definitions of 'work'. By passive labour I refer to ways in which different participants in such activities may conceive of their roles such as healthy volunteering as 'non-work'. This is because these activities may not fit with normative definitions of work, as the roles do not involve physically and actively doing something to produces value; yet they produce value for the industry. This relates to how work takes place and is organised in spaces commonly ignored as sites of work in post-Fordist economies as outlined by Cooper and Waldby, coupled with the increasing casualization of work, in what is now referred to as the '"gig" economy'. The gig economy is a growing labour market in which people are employed in short and zero hour contracts, paid minimum wage or less, and have no formal employee protections associated with workers' rights. People in these situations are often categorised as self-employed and are thus responsible for their own safety and welfare, while absolving their 'employers' of any contractual responsibility except for paying the agreed fee (Booth 2017; Wilson 2017). This has left many people in vulnerable and exploitative situations. In many ways, healthy volunteers fit in this category, except that their work does not involve physical labour but merely being present in body. Another difference would be that they are paid relatively more compared to those employed on such contracts in other industries such as courier and delivery firms. However, they are all involved in these varied forms of labour at their own risk.

Specifically, for healthy volunteers, it is how inactivity is seen as pointless and yet is crucial to the creation of value for corporate pharmaceutical industries that is of interest in this discussion. This view of inactivity and the body relates to Marx's views on fetishism (Marx 1961); specifically, how the production of value often overlooks the social relations in which value is produced but focuses on the 'objects' being exchanged for money—in this case, to use Leder's (1990) term, bodies become absent or invisible. The bodies of participants become mere tools for value production and often talked of as invisible parts of the process. In addition, whereas in Fordism, labour is mainly dependent on manual contributions of labourers, healthy volunteering becomes passive labour as participants do not have to do any manual work. Instead, their bodies become sites on which work is done and thus value is created. Similarly, as Marx views value to be created by those lacking means of production, healthy volunteers are equally those in financially straitened situations lacking the means of production and subsistence. Therefore, in passive labour, work is no longer reliant on the manual contribution of those involved in value creation; rather, it is based on the body itself. In this case, labour is provided by subjecting the body to experiments in clinical drug trials, which create profit-generating medicines for pharmaceutical companies, rather than by manual work. However, similarly as in manual labour, those involved in passive labour are those lacking the means of subsistence. In addition, healthy volunteering can be seen as unskilled flexible labour and in this case participants are seen as independent contractors (Elliot 2014), and involvement is to some extent at their own risk.

More concerning today, healthy volunteering has become routine among some groups, particularly those in financially straitened situations. The work of Abadie, Fisher, and, Tishler and Bartholomae among others in the US shows how some healthy volunteers have come to see their bodies and body parts as resources with which to make a living. It is here that questions about what constitutes an acceptable way of making a living and individual agency collide. Given the commercial prospects of the human body in clinical drug trials, there has been an increase in debates around the role of the human subjects or their bodies. Of interest, here is the fact that in market exchanges, goods swap hands and ownership, whereas in clinical drug trials, healthy volunteers retain the ownership, control, and responsibility of the body while sharing or lending their bodies for research. In addition, as noted in Hochschild's (1983) work, emotional labour is also relevant here as healthy volunteers do not just offer their bodies for research, but make various kinds of emotional commitments ranging from reluctant money-seeking to being 'friendly with staff'. This adds to what I call varieties of 'passivity' in different types of 'labour'. The term passive labour is used here as it can be applied to social phenomenon such as art and fashion modelling, where participation solely depends on the body and rarely involves physical activities.

Views of the body as a commodity possessed by autonomous individuals is of concern to medical sociologists. This is because conceiving human subjects as a valuable'resource' is symptomatic of consumerist, neoliberal tendencies which focuses primarily on free markets, individual liberties, and reduced state regulation (Scheper-Hughes 2000; Sharp 2000). Neoliberal approaches are prevalent in healthcare in the UK, illustrated by the growth of the CRO industry; the emphasis is on choice and the emerging debate about capitalisation of healthcare in which patients are regarded as consumers. Understanding healthy volunteering requires an awareness of how the conduct and regulation of clinical drug trials is influenced by the neoliberal approach, which extends beyond privatisation to include the commodification of the body. Discussions about healthy volunteers are framed within ideas of liberty and consumption while limiting options for the individual with a discourse of altruism and gift relationship, volunteering, rationality, and efficiency. At an institutional level, healthy volunteers become consumers or even individual contractors, as pointed out earlier. However, such an approach masks the suffering and pain endured by many who subject themselves to these trials and obscures the value of the exchanges. Neoliberalism espouses a view of capable, rational, and free individual. Allowing the body to be used in exchange for payment is justified; healthy volunteers are seen as capable, consenting adults who should be allowed to do whatever they wish. Viewing human subjects as rational actors negates the effect of unequal power and disadvantages in trial processes. There is also the assumption that all players have equal access to resources and influence and thus take part in the market on an equal footing with everyone else (Massey 2013).

Another aspect to healthy volunteer involvement in clinical drug trials is how it relates to Scott's (1977) idea of moral economy of the peasant. Scott draws attention to the peasants' need to produce enough to support their families while meeting the social expectations of their society and the risks attendant with survival. Scott explored the struggles of peasants during years of famine in Burma and Vietnam in the 1930s when they demanded access to land, the right to glean on farmlands, and fair market prices. A parallel can be drawn with the ways in which people are living on the margins in the UK today, obviously within a neoliberal context. Social expectations can influence how people respond to social problems such as unemployment, loss of jobs, or even extreme poverty. Questions about healthy volunteering therefore are taken to be ethical questions about how institutions use human subjects in medical research, asking whether it is right to encourage people to engage with risk by paying them significant sums. Nevertheless, the morality of healthy volunteers is also often questioned by society: why are they so willing to subject their bodies to such risks for the monetary reward offered? Answering these questions requires looking beyond consent and capability, to consider the wider social context in which such decisions take place.

Summary

This chapter drew attention to how rational choice theories and their conceptions of individuals as rational actors have influenced the principles and practice of bioethics, apparent in the practice of clinical drug trials today. While the intention of bioethics was to restore dignity and agency to individuals, the policy actions have had unintended consequences—blind spots in the interaction among agency, power, and inequality and their capacity to shape each other. Theories of economics, rational choice, and motivation are conceived to be a result of people's expressed wants and goals which influence their behaviour or actions. Bioethics applies the rational choice theory in its classic sense, emphasising individual capacity for voluntary action, and assumes people's capability to make informed decisions. Thus, the assumption that adequate provision of information is sufficient to answer ethical questions arising from healthy volunteering. Information provision is regarded as liberating and enables individuals make'informed' decisions (Corrigan 2003).

However, ethical considerations in healthy volunteering should go beyond this utilitarian view to consider broader aspects of decision-making. This is because, while individuals may be making choices within this framework, rational choice approaches negate the complex interplay of the individual and the wider social and political structures and how these create a milieu in which certain forms of actions are preferable for certain social groups. Neither model accounts for the ways in which power relationships and wider social factors such as employment, income, and cost of living, debts, and social expectations come together to make certain course of actions, such as taking part in clinical drug trials, attractive. Furthermore, in portraying individuals as calculative and focused on financial benefits, this view does not consider actions motivated by norms or routine such as altruism. To understand people's involvement in clinical drug trials requires an approach that considers individual action broadly, without focusing exclusively on issues of risk and reward.

References

Abadie, R. (2010). *The professional guinea pig: Big pharma and the risky world of human subjects*. London: Duke University Press.

Adams, J., & Hillman, M. (2001). Bicycle helmets: risk taking is influenced by people's perception of safety and danger. *BMJ: British Medical Journal, 322*(7293), 1063.

Adams, J., & Hillman, M. (2001). The risk compensation theory and bicycle helmets. *Injury Prevention, 7*(2), 89–91.

Beauchamp, T. L., & Childress, J. F. (2001). *Principles of biomedical ethics*. Oxford: Oxford University Press.

Beck, U. (1992). *Risk society: Towards a new modernity* (Vol. 17). London: Sage.

Becker, G. S. (1963). Rational action and economic theory: a reply to I. Kirzner. *Journal of Political Economy, 71*(1), 82–83.

Becker, G. S. (1993). Nobel lecture: The economic way of looking at behavior. *Journal of Political Economy, 101*(3), 385–409.

Bentley, J. P., & Thacker, P. G. (2004). The influence of risk and monetary payment on the research participation decision making process. *Journal of Medical Ethics, 30*(3), 293–298.

Bloor, M. (1995). *The sociology of HIV transmission*. London: Sage.

Bond, C., et al. (2012). "It had to be my choice": Indigenous smoking cessation and negotiations of risk, resistance and resilience. *Health, Risk & Society, 14*(6), 565–581.

Booth, R. (2017). £1.74 an hour: Jinn couriers complain over low earnings. *The Guardian*. https://www.theguardian.com/business/2017/feb/13/125-for-72-hours-work-jinn-couriers-complain-over-low-earnings?CMP=oth_b-aplnews_d-2. Accessed 13 Feb 2017.

Bosk, C. L. (1999). Professional ethicist available: Logical, secular, friendly. *Daedalus, 128*(4), 47–68.

Brown, P., & Calnan, M. (2010). The risks of managing ncertainty: The limitations of governance and choice, and the potential for trust. *Social Policy and Society, 9*(1), 13–24.

Campbell, C. (1996). On the concept of motive in sociology. *Sociology, 30*(1), 101–114.

Corrigan, O. (2003). Empty ethics: The problem with informed consent. *Sociology of Health & Illness, 25*(7), 768–792.

Devine, E. G., et al. (2013). Concealment and fabrication by experienced research subjects. *Clinical Drug Trials, 10*(6), 935–948.

Dingwall, R. (2008). The ethical case against ethical regulation in humanities and social science research. *Twenty-First Century Society, 3*(1), 1–12.

Elliott, C. (2014, July 28). The best-selling, billion-dollar pills tested on homeless people: How the destitute and the mentally ill are being used as human

lab rats. *Medium*, July 28. https://medium.com/matter/did-big-pharma-test-your-meds-on-homeless-people-a6d8d3fc7dfe.
Evans, J. H. (2000). A sociological account of the growth of principlism. *Hastings Center Report, 30*(5), 31–39.
Fiorino, D. J. (1990). Citizen participation and environmental risk: A survey of institutional mechanisms. *Science, Technology and Human Values, 15*(2), 226–243.
Fisher, J. A. (2007). Coming soon to a physician near you: Medical neoliberalism and pharmaceutical clinical drug trials. *Harvard Health Policy Review: A Student Publication of the Harvard Interfaculty Initiative in Health Policy, 8*(1), 61.
Fisher, J. A. (2009). *Medical research for hire: The political economy of pharmaceutical clinical drug trials.* New Brunswick: Rutgers University Press.
Fisher, J. A. (2015). Feeding and bleeding: The institutional banalization of risk to healthy volunteers in phase I pharmaceutical clinical drug trials. *Science, Technology and Human Values, 40*(2), 199–226.
Geissler, P. W. (2011). "Transport to where?" Reflections on the problem of value and time à propos an awkward practice in medical research. *Journal of Cultural Economy, 4*(1), 45–64.
Giddens, A. (1991). *Modernity and self-identity: self and society in the late modern age.* Cambridge: Polity Press.
Giddens, A. (2013). *The consequences of modernity.* Hoboken: Wiley.
Glickman, S. W., et al. (2009). Ethical and scientific implications of the globalization of clinical research. *New England Journal of Medicine, 360*, 816–823.
Green, J. (2009). Is it time for the sociology of health to abandon "risk"? *Health, Risk & Society, 11*(6), 493–508.
Harris, Y., et al. (1996). Why African Americans may not be participating in clinical drug trials. *Journal of the National Medical Association, 88*(10), 630.
Hazelgrove, J. (2002). The old faith and the new science: The nuremberg code and human experimentation ethics in Britain, 1946–1973. *Social History of Medicine, 15*(1), 109–135.
Hedgecoe, A. (2004). Critical bioethics: Beyond the social science critique of applied ethics. *Bioethics, 18*(2), 120–143.
Hillman, M. (1993). Cycling and the promotion of health. *Policy Studies, 14*(2), 49–58.
Hillman, M., Adams, J., & Whitelegg, J. (1990). One false move. London: Policy Studies Institute.
Hobson-West, P. (2003). Understanding vaccination resistance: Moving beyond risk. *Health, Risk & Society, 5*(3), 273–283.
Hochschild, A. R. (1983). *The managed heart.* Berkeley: University of California Press.
Hoeyer, K. (2009). Informed consent: The making of a ubiquitous rule in medical practice. *Organization, 16*(2), 267–288.
Horlick-Jones, T. (2004). Experts in risk? Do they exist? *Health, Risk & Society, 6*(2), 107–114.
Horlick-Jones, T. (2005). Informal logics of risk: Contingency and modes of practical reasoning. *Journal of Risk Research, 8*(3), 253–272.

Leder, D. (1990). *The absent body*. Chicago: University of Chicago Press.
Lemmens, T., & Elliott, C. (1999). Guinea pigs on the payroll: The ethics of paying research subjects. *Accountability in Research, 7*(1), 3–20.
Lupton, D. (2000). Foucault and the Medicalisation Critique. In A. Petersen & R. Bunton (Eds.). *Foucault: Health and Medicine*. New York: Routledge.
Lyng, S. (2005). *Edgework: The sociology of risk-taking*. London: Routledge.
Lyng, S. (2009 [2008]). Edgework, risk, and uncertainty. In J. Zinn (Ed.). *Social Theories of Risk and Uncertainty: An Introduction* (pp. 106–135). Oxford: Blackwell.
M⊘ldrup, C., & Morgall, J. M. (2001). Risk society: Reconsidered in a drug context. *Health, Risk & Society, 3*(1): 59–74.
Marx, K. (1961). Economic and Philosophical Manuscripts. *Eric Fromm, Marx's Concept of Man*. New York: Frederick Ungar. Available at http://www.912freedomlibrary.org/custom-1/Economic%20and%20Philosophical%20Manuscripts,%20The%20-%20Karl%20Marx%20(1932)%20BM%20Act%20OEF%209.330.pdf.
Massey, D. (2013) Vocabuarlies of the economy. In S. Hall, D. Massey, & M. Rustin (Eds.), *After neoliberalism? The Kilburn Manifeston*. Soundings. http://www.lwbooks.co.uk/journals/soundings/manifesto.html.
Milgram, S. (1963). Behavioral study of obedience. *The Journal of Abnormal and Social Psychology, 67*(4), 371.
Mills, C. W. (1940). Situated actions and vocabularies of motive. *American Sociological Review, 5*(6), 904–913.
Mishra, A., & Graham, J. E. (2012). Risk, choice and the "girl vaccine": Unpacking Human Papillomavirus (HPV) immunisation. *Health, Risk & Society, 14*(1), 57–69.
Moser, D. J., et al. (2004). Coercion and informed consent in research involving prisoners. *Comprehensive Psychiatry, 45*(1), 1–9.
O'Neill, O. (2003). Some limits of informed consent. *Journal of Medical Ethics, 29*(1), 4–7.
Peretti-Watel, P., & Moatti, J. (2006). Understanding risk behaviours: How the sociology of deviance may contribute? The case of drug-taking. *Social Science and Medicine, 63*(3), 675–679.
Peretti-Watel, P., et al. (2007). 'Smoking too few cigarettes to be at risk? Smokers' perceptions of risk and risk denial, a French survey. *Tobacco Control, 16*(5), 351–356.
Petryna, A. (2005). Ethical variability: Drug development and globalizing clinical drug trials. *American Ethnologist, 32*(2), 183–197.
Petryna, A. (2009). *When experiments travel: Clinical drug trials and the global search for human subjects*. Princeton: Princeton University Press.
Poltorak, M., Leach, M., & Fairhead, J. (2004). *MMR "choices" in Brighton: Understanding public engagement with vaccination science and delivery*. Monograph. January. Available at http://www.ids.ac.uk/files/Wp224.pdf.

Rajan, K. S. (2006). *Biocapital: The constitution of postgenomic life*. Durham: Duke University Press.
Roberts, E. F. S., & Scheper-Hughes, N. (2011). Introduction: Medical migrations. *Body & Society, 17*(2–3), 1–30.
Rogers, A., & Pilgrim, D. (1995). The risk of resistance perspectives on the mass childhood immunisation programme. In J. Gabe (Ed.). *Sociology of Health & Illness Monograph Series* (pp. 73–90).
Royal College of Physicians. (1986). Research on healthy volunteers. *Journal of the Royal College of Physicians, 20*, 243–257.
Scheper-Hughes, N. (2000). The global traffic in human organs1. *Current Anthropology, 41*(2), 191–224.
Scocozza, L. (1989). Ethics and medical science. On voluntary participation in biomedical experimentation. *Acta Sociologica 32*(3), 283–293.
Scott, J. C. (1977). *The moral economy of the peasant: Rebellion and subsistence in Southeast Asia*. New Haven: Yale University Press.
Scott, R. (2000). Rational choice theory. In *Understanding contemporary society: Theories of the present*, (pp. 126–138).
Sharp, L. A. (2000). The commodification of the body and its parts. *Annual Review of Anthropology, 29*, 287–328.
Taylor-Goody, P., & Zinn, J. O. (2006). Current directions in risk research: New developments in psychology and sociology. *Risk Analysis, 26*(2), 397–411.
Tulloch, J., & Lupton, D. (2003). *Risk and everyday life*. Sage.
Waldby, C. (2002). Stem cells, tissue cultures and the production of biovalue. *Health, 6*(3), 305–323.
Walls, J., et al. (2004). Critical trust: Understanding lay perceptions of health and safety risk regulation. *Health, Risk & Society, 6*(2), 133–150.
Washington, H. A. (2006). *Medical apartheid: The dark history of medical experimentation on Black Americans from colonial times to the present*. New York: Doubleday.
Weber, M. (1978). Basic sociological terms. *Economy and Society, 1*, 3–62.
Weindling, P. (2001). The origins of nformed consent: The international scientific commission on medical war crimes, and the nuremberg code. *Bulletin of the History of Medicine, 75*(1), 37–71.
Weinstein, M. (2001). A public culture for guinea pigs: US human research subjects after the Tuskegee study. *Science as Culture, 10*(2), 195–223.
Will, C. M. (2011). Mutual benefit, added value? *Journal of Cultural Economy, 4*(1), 11–26.
Wilson, J., & Musick, M. (1999). The effects of volunteering on the volunteer. *Law and contemporary problems, 62*(4), 141–168.
Wilson, B. (2017). What is the 'gig' economy? *BBC Business News*, February 10. http://www.bbc.co.uk/news/business-38930048.
Wynne, B. (1996). May the sheep safely graze? A reflexive view of the expert-lay knowledge divide. In S. Lash, B. Szerszynski, & B. Wynne (Eds.), *Risk, envrionment and modernity: Towards a new ecoclogy*. London: Sage.

CHAPTER 3

Risk, Motivation and Decision-making in Everyday Life: A Phenomenological Approach

Abstract This chapter provides an alternative perspective to the views influencing bioethics, namely the Schutzian phenomenological concept of systems of relevance, as a tool for exploring individuals' motivation and decision-making. I show how both individual, wider institutional, and sociopolitical, and economic contexts play a part in individual decision-making. Specifically, I illustrate complexities in the relationship between financial rewards, risk, and individual rationality. Schutz calls for sociological attention to how the context in which decisions and actions take place intersect to influence decisions.

Keywords Risk · Relevance · Volunteering · Social context
Phenomenology · Institutions · Individual motivations

Why a Phenomenological Approach?

So far, I have highlighted the theoretical concepts and substantive debates that have shaped views of healthy volunteering. I argue that while monetary incentives could be a motivation for taking part in clinical drug trials, discussions about why people take part in clinical drug trials mainly focus on patient groups, who are predominantly portrayed as altruistic or treatment-seeking volunteers. There has been insufficient interrogation of the contexts and circumstances in which people make decisions to get into healthy volunteering in the UK. Where healthy volunteers have been considered, with notable exceptions, they have

S. Mwale, *Healthy Volunteers in Commercial Clinical Drug Trials*,
DOI 10.1007/978-3-319-59214-5_3

been conflated with patient groups. Such studies have portrayed healthy volunteers as mainly motivated by altruism: desiring to help the development of science in its quest to find remedies for the ever-increasing numbers of incurable diseases. Of interest, here is how the role of financial incentives, while acknowledged as an issue, has rarely been problematized or interrogated.

Anthropological and sociological literature on global offshoring of clinical drug trials shows how people in diverse socioeconomic and sociopolitical contexts in the 'Global South' take part in clinical drug trials. Another criticism of bioethics framework with regard to healthy volunteering is linked to therapeutic misconception and justice (Appelbaum et al. 2008; Lidz and Appelbaum 2002). In this context, structural inequalities in access to healthcare and income constrain the choices of populations in the Global South, particularly in poorly organised and underdeveloped healthcare systems in countries such as Brazil and India (Petryna 2004; Rajan 2006), where people take part in clinical drug trials to access healthcare. However, it is also important to apply a sociological analysis on the presumed wealthy 'Global North', where involvement in clinical drug trials is seen to be purely a matter of choice. It is important to interrogate the context in which people take part in clinical drug trials and how perceptions of choice and freedom framed within neoliberal terms in the West, obscure the socioeconomic and sociopolitical conditions that make healthy volunteering a worthwhile option.

Without testing the patience of the reader, I would like to restate here that central to issues faced by bioethics with regard to healthy volunteering is the fact that bioethics principles of rational consent and voluntarism are rendered redundant by incentives, particularly when dealing with questions of risk and uncertainty. The overreliance on rational and economic theoretical approaches to risk and concepts of individuals in ethical policy considerations within bioethics results in a negation of the social context in which rationality and choice are practiced. The limitation of these theoretical approaches in explaining risk and motivation, especially in clinical drug trials contexts, is a tendency to overemphasize capability; it assumes rationality takes place in a vacuum, as everyone in society is thought to have equal access to resources. Furthermore, there is a negation of the structural and institutional impact such as the socioeconomic and sociopolitical context on people's motivation to engage with risk. Therefore, these approaches are not useful in explaining behaviours or actions that may be habitual and repetitive in nature (actions for which people normally would not require much prior thought or calculation).

Consequently, to better understand human involvement in clinical drug trials, there is a need to consider the relationship between subjective and institutional contexts in which people engage with risk. Although the idea that people take rational actions has been widely recognised in sociology and beyond, within sociology it is acknowledged that people engage in both rational and nonrational actions. To understand why people become guinea pigs requires an approach that considers the role of habituation, emotions, and other dimensions underlying human action such as beliefs, personal financial circumstances, and so on and how these are shaped and mediated by institutional influences. A phenomenological approach enables such an analysis.

Phenomenology: Motivation, Risk Perception, and Social Constraints

A phenomenological perspective on social action focuses on actions that are often unconsidered and taken for granted. From a phenomenological perspective, such actions typically are seen as routine and involve 'the suspension of these unconsidered certitudes and an explicit analytical interest in the previously implicit' (Bloor 1995, 97). Using this approach in analysing human involvement in clinical drug trials critiques views of the 'decision' and our understanding of how decisions to take part in clinical drug trials are made. This social arena of unconsidered actions, beliefs, and unspoken understandings is what Alfred Schutz (1970, 139) refers to as the 'world of routine activities'—of familiar topics, conversations, habitual expectations, and routine behaviour (Bloor 1995). Some motivations for engaging with risk may be calculative, such as volunteering with the purpose of receiving money to pay off debt, but volunteering in clinical drug trials with other motivations and without any prior calculation also happens routinely and repeatedly, with relatively little reflection. For instance, Abadie (2010) argues that people who take part in clinical drug trials as healthy volunteers often do not consider other options available to them. The tension between calculative and routine action is Schutz's main interest. Similar discussions can also be seen in the work of

Bourdieu (1990) on attention and habituation. Therefore, exploring the 'taken for granted' can be linked to what Back (2015) refers to as 'sociology of the everyday'. Back argues that ordinary everyday life should be taken seriously by exploring 'what is at stake in our daily encounters with… people' around us and to 'think of the wider spectrum of life experiences from the despair and social change to the ordinary triumphs of getting by' (Back 2015, 821). In doing so, we gain a better understanding of the contexts in which daily life struggles and inequalities take place. Therefore, seeing that healthy volunteering now happens in a 'life-as-usual' manner, a sociological attention to human involvement in clinical drug trials provides a space to move the smallest of social issues that may otherwise be considered routine into a story of larger social significance. A phenomenological approach used in this way brings to the fore issues that would otherwise stay hidden in the 'mundane aspects of everyday life' and transforms the ordinary into live and significant issues worthy of social and political attention (Back 2015, 821).

It is attention to such aspects of daily life that is of interest to Schutz. For Schutz, the distinction between familiarisation and thoughtfulness occurs because of the changes in thinking that happen when individuals are repeatedly confronted with similar incentives. When faced with a new situation, people may take time to think through the available courses of action. Not all options available will be suitable; some decisions may be delayed until one course is considered appropriate. However, with routine activities, the complex cognitive processes fail; an individual must make a rapid appraisal of the problem and take action without much consideration of other options. A contrast can be drawn between the first decision (e.g., to volunteer) which might be polythetic and 'rational', and subsequent similar decisions that would be monothetic, but knowingly based on the previous polythetic decision. Having decided at first that it would be a good idea to volunteer, subsequent acts of volunteering can be done with little or no thought. This illustrates how cognition is both a polythetic (step-wise) process and a monothetic (single flash) process (Bloor 1995, 97). Polythetic decision-making can be seen in theories of behaviour that focus on the cost–benefit analysis (Schutz 1970) of risk-taking. Much as cost–benefit analysis may be helpful in explaining behaviour, it does not take into account the different contexts in which decisions are made. Therefore, understanding risk-taking behaviour requires an exploratory framework encompassing both the new and the routine in the decision-making process of social interactions.

For Schutz this can be achieved by using a 'system of relevances', which collates a variety of perceptive activities within one framework. This refers to how individuals position and make sense of social problems. The systems of relevance comprises topical, interpretive, and motivational relevances (Schutz and Luckmann 1974). These are divided into subcategories depending on whether the stimulus is volitional (intrinsic) or imposed. Each of Schutz's relevances can be extended depending on one's interest in the activity and the extent to which one may be familiar with the stimuli (Schutz 1970; Bloor 1995). Relevances are determined by the biographical situation, which Schutz refers to as how one's response, views and beliefs to social stimuli are shaped by the social contexts and how we are socialised into these spaces. Experiences in our social contexts provide the source and the stock of knowledge needed to make decisions (Schutz and Luckmann 1974).

Topical Relevances

Topical relevances define whether an issue at hand is problematic and worthy of an interpretation by the individual. Topical relevance comes into play when something does not fit prior knowledge or expectations and thus the topic or issue becomes relevant to an individual. In other words, topical relevance arises when things become questionable to the individual, and this happens for certain specific reasons (Goettlich 2011). Intrinsic topical relevances denote the voluntary quest for interpretation, while the imposed stimuli denote the constraints. The extent to which an issue becomes topically relevant depends on previous knowledge, experiences, and the degree of uncertainty the situation brings. For instance, a woman who has grown up knowing that using an intradermal implant is the best form of contraception goes to her doctor and requests one. After the assessment, the doctor inserts the implant. Until this stage, the implant as a form of contraception is not topically relevant, according to Schutz's terminology. However, after having the implant, she is asked in a conversation with another friend if she had done some research before deciding on this form of contraception. Had she considered its potential side effects and general safety? At this point the implant becomes topically relevant: she becomes uncertain about the safety of the implant and starts to question her actions; hence the need for interpretation (interpretive relevance).

Interpretive Relevance

Interpretative relevances refer to the restricted knowledge the individual may possess regarding the issue at hand and to aspects of topical relevance which need an interpretation or further understanding; this is because not every aspect of the subject might need understanding. Similarly, only the interpretive relevance of the stock of knowledge defines what part of the stock of knowledge to use in the interpretation. The individual may draw on previous experience and knowledge to interpret the uncertainty that the encounter brings. Using the earlier example of the implant, the woman may begin to ask what the implications are if the implant becomes harmful to her health, and what that might mean for her life in general. In seeking to understand the situation, the individual may conclude that the implant is safe and that there is no need to worry about it. Alternatively, the individual may become more uncertain about its safety and even question her decision to have an implant in the first place. At this stage, the implant becomes motivationally relevant (Schutz 1970).

Motivational Relevance

Motivational relevance denotes what Weber (1968) refers to as the 'adequate grounds' upon which human behaviour is based. Schutz, to an extent, espouses Weber's notion, but sees motives as composed of 'in order to' and 'because of' motives. 'In order to' motives generally refer to 'because of' motives after one has taken an action concerned with the future and yet building on past experiences or knowledge (Schutz 1970). The process of interpretation and taking steps to deal with the situation is complex and does not follow the order outlined in this section. Decisions may sometimes be kept on hold while other options are investigated so that competing or conflicting options can be discarded. On the other hand, the process can be momentary, due to marginal interest in the matter (which can involve the category of motivational relevances) and because of an individual's pre-existing familiarity with the situation. This results in the individual drifting into a monothetic mode of thinking (Bloor 1995). Again, to use the example of the implant, the woman might decide that there is no need to worry as there are many other women who have implants and they are well; or she may simply trust the doctor's explanations about the safety of the implant. On the other hand, she may have all the available information about safety risks associated with implants but still decide to have the implant because she prefers it to contraceptive pills, or she is convinced that the side effects will not affect her. Alternatively, the woman might reconsider the information regarding risk and ask to have it removed. This illustrates one framework for understanding the decision-making process and how decisions are sometimes based on limited information and made without much prior thought.

The system of relevance has been used in sociological research in different contexts. For instance, Bloor's (1995) research on the sociology of HIV transmission used this approach to explore the contexts in which decisions involving risk among gay male prostitutes take place. He found that in most cases decisions are shaped by an interplay of personal factors such as an individual's ability to handle a client, or a tendency to want to avoid conflict with the client. All these aspects were crucial in shaping responses to HIV infection risks in these contexts.

The earlier discussion illustrates the investigative significance of Schutz's system in the conceptualisation of motivation and risk perception. One of the merits of using the system is that it draws attention to the circumstances in which action takes place instead of the preconceptions the individual brings to the situation. This provides a good basis for exploring volunteering in clinical drug trials, not only from an individual perspective, but also considering the wider sociopolitical and socioeconomic milieu in which volunteering takes place. The system also highlights the distinctions between polythetic and monothetic decision-making processes, and volitional and imposed dichotomies which are often unaddressed in theoretical explanations of motivations and risk perception. Using Schutz's system of relevances and considering both volitional and imposed dimensions of action enables us to observe how individual circumstances interact with institutional or structural influences in the context of volunteering for clinical drug trials.

The Individual and Structural Elements of Schutz's System of Relevances

One of the criticisms of Schutz's approach is that it is overly subjective in its perspective on human action. However, the theory of the system of relevances does suggest structural considerations. As discussed earlier, Schutz considers both volitional and imposed aspects of motivation underlying human action. The imposed aspect here implies outside influences or pressures. I am particularly interested in institutional or structural influences such as socioeconomic circumstances and how they affect the decision-making process among healthy volunteers. In this case, a phenomenological approach to institutional theory provides the structural analysis for the discussion.

The notion of institutional forces or pressures refers to forms of social action or rules that have been established over time. These involve both bodies of knowledge and sometimes even actual organisations; for example, bioethics as a discipline brings biology, health, and ethics together to provide a framework for understanding the moral implications of human participation in clinical drug trials, while regulators (both scientific experts and research ethics committees [REC]), advisory groups, and other organisations have emerged to consider the moral and rational dimensions of volunteering. Institutional considerations within phenomenological institutional theory consider the ways in which structures, rules, systems, norms, and routines become normative and influential guidelines for social behaviour (DiMaggio and Powell 1991). The focus therefore is twofold. On one hand, sociologists are encouraged to consider the taken-for-granted aspects of everyday life, particularly with regard to engaging with risk. On the other hand, it is important to analyse how institutions are organised and how wider institutional structures contour individual decisions and actions. This facilitates a nuanced understanding of human behaviour, including how it is produced and sustained by particular social norms, rules, and types of actors. Using this approach means taking the conduct, organisation, and regulation of healthy volunteering as an ensemble of individual and institutional/technical aspects embedded within established ethical, sociopolitical, and socioeconomic contexts. The approach requires considering institutions as complex and powerful in nature (Avgerou 2003) while remaining attentive to the subdued voices within and outside these structures and how the systems in place propagate, define, and influence social norms and daily life experiences (Walker et al. 2012).

Thus, questions about motivations and decision-making require consideration of not only individual reasons for actions, but also how institutional motivations, or interests, drive policies and approaches to business, and structure functions of institutions (Douglas 1987). To understand how institutions operate, shape, and view healthy volunteers' experiences, and the phenomenological approach to institutional theory, requires greater attention to the significance of the symbolic and power facets of institutions. This is because institutions are not just technical systems; they also contour social spaces, including individuals in and around them (Scott 1987).

Rather than adopting a utilitarian perspective, which takes the premise that individuals always pursue their own interests, taking a phenomenological approach entails considering how individuals and institutions interact and refocuses attention on taken-for-granted factors such as norms, assumptions, and social circumstances that delineate people's actions. This should not be taken as a disavowal of the reality of purposive actions by institutions or individuals, but rather as a demonstration of ways in which people's actions are shaped and defined by interactions between institutions and individuals. In taking a phenomenological approach in this book, I highlight aspects of healthy volunteers' lives that are often taken for granted or may be obscured by the discourse of voluntarism and consent. I show how their decisions to become human guinea pigs take place in a space imbued with unequal power relations and interest which need considering when explaining healthy volunteering.

Summary

This subject under discussion here is situated at the connexion of the individual and the institution in phase 1 drug trials. I put forward a dialogue of how individuals and institutions interact to shape experiences in and views of healthy volunteering. Using a phenomenological approach, particularly Schutz's concept of a system of relevances, is useful for illuminating how both healthy volunteering and institutions context interact to result in certain perceptions or risk and rationality. This framework provides an analysis that considers government, corporate organisations, and professional expertise, how they view individuals and their bodies, and how they define customs and practices. This framework is useful because the business of clinical drug trials takes place in a space of interdependent but varied organisations and actors interdependencies. Rational consent, volunteering, and monetary incentives, along with the wider socioeconomic and sociopolitical context are all ultimately dimensions of human involvement in clinical drug trials. Unlike rational choice theory and bioethics principles of rational consent and voluntarism, understanding human involvement in clinical drug trials requires a consideration of both subjective and structural contexts. To do this, a phenomenological approach drawing on Schutz' framework system of relevances is used, as it helps identify key actors and agencies, and their relations, and therefore is useful for analysing the institutions and practice of phase I clinical drug trials.

So far, I have shown how healthy volunteering involves an interplay of social, commercial, and political actors who influence each other and the conduct of and experiences in clinical drug trials. To understand healthy volunteer motivations and experiences in clinical drug trials, there is need to consider how individual circumstances such as socioeconomics and relationships with others and institutions influence decision-making.

References

Abadie, R. (2010). *The professional guinea pig: Big pharma and the risky world of human subjects*. London: Duke University Press.

Appelbaum, P., et al. (2008). Twenty-five years of therapeutic misconception. *The Hastings Center Report, 38*(2), 5–7.

Avgerou, C. (2003). *IT as an institutional actor in developing countries*. Burlington, VT: Ashgate.

Back, L. (2015). Why everyday life matters: Class, community and making life livable. *Sociology, 49*(5), 820–836.

Bloor, M. (1995). *The sociology of HIV transmission*. London: SAGE.

Bourdieu, P. (1990). *The logic of practice*. Palo Alto: Stanford University Press.

DiMaggio, P. J., & Powell, W. W. (1991). Introduction. In W. W. Powell & P. J. DiMaggio (Eds.), *The new institutionalism in organizational analysis*. London: The University of Chicago Press.

Douglas, M. (1987). *How institutions think*. London: Routledge & Kegan Paul.

Goettlich, A. (2011). Power and powerlessness: Alfred Schutz's theory of relevance and its possible impact on a sociological analysis of power. *Civitas–Revista de Ciências Sociais, 11*(3), 491–508.

Lidz, C. W., & Appelbaum, P. S. (2002). The therapeutic misconception: Problems and solutions. *Medical Care, 40*(9), V55–V63.

Petryna, A. (2004). Biological citizenship: The science and politics of Chernobyl-exposed populations. *Osiris, 19*, 250–265. doi:10.2307/3655243.

Rajan, K. S. (2006). *Biocapital: The constitution of postgenomic life*. Durham: Duke University Press.

Schutz, A. (1970). *Reflections on the problem of relevance* (R. M. Zaner, Trans.). New Haven: Yale University Press.

Schutz, A., & Luckmann, T. (1974). *The structures of the life-world* (H. T. Engelhardt & R. M. Zaner, Trans.). London: Heinemann.

Scott, W. R. (1987). The adolescence of institutional theory. *Administrative Science Quarterly, 32*(4), 493–511.
Walker, C., et al. (2012). *Responsible individuals and irresponsible institutions? A report into mental health and the UK credit industry*. Brighton: University of Brighton.
Weber, M. (1968). *Economy and Society*. New York: Bedmnster Press.

CHAPTER 4

Who Takes Part in Clinical Drug Trials?

Abstract Drawing on statistical data, this chapter illustrates the considerable variations in the backgrounds of healthy volunteers. I present the demographic profiles of healthy volunteers and introduce the relationship between income, financial rewards, and financial security. I illustrate how healthy volunteering in the UK may not be delineated purely as the preserve of marginalised and unemployed individuals. Rather, based on the sample used in the research informing this book, it appears that healthy volunteers in the UK are mostly employed in full-time and relatively well-paid jobs. I argue that healthy volunteer involvement should be seen in the context of rising costs of living and that this makes taking part in clinical drug trials a worthwhile option for some people.

Keywords Clinical drug trials · Healthy volunteers · Demographics
Volunteering · Income

Significance of Healthy Volunteer Demographics in Clinical Drug Trials

Demographics are the characteristics that define a population. These include, but not limited to, the following: age, gender, occupation, level of educational achievement, and address. In clinical drug trials, especially in the US, demographic profiles for patient groups who take part

S. Mwale, *Healthy Volunteers in Commercial Clinical Drug Trials*,
DOI 10.1007/978-3-319-59214-5_4

in clinical drug trials are easily available. For instance, the US Centre for Information and Study on Clinical Research Participation (CISCRP) has information on numbers of patients and their age, gender, and ethnicity; nonetheless, concerning healthy volunteers in the UK, well-documented demographic profiles for healthy volunteers in early phase studies are not available. While CROs may have this information, it is certainly not available for public scrutiny.

In social and medical research, particularly in clinical drug trials, demographics are vital as they help to structure trial design and the recruitment of participants for research (Frank 2004). Precise demographic information (for example, age, gender, employment, and educational attainment) is key to successful research for pharmaceutical companies because it influences planning, distribution, and marketing strategies of their products as well. CROs have managed to build successful business based on their ability to quickly access and recruit target populations for clinical drug testing. This is because adequate numbers of volunteers are considered essential for robust evidence and wider testing of medicines.

A historical analysis and current research of clinical trial demographics in the US (see Epstein 2008; Tishler and Bartholomae 2002, 2003; Abadie 2010; Fisher 2007 cited earlier) reveals disparities in representation of marginalised groups in clinical research and the ramifications of such unequal representation. If consideration is not given to who takes part in clinical drug trials, then certain groups are bound to be exposed to exploitative recruitment; they may also have little say in their protection from undue risk or exploitation and lack advice and support in the trial process. Well-defined demographic data about healthy volunteers enrich debates about their involvement in clinical drug trials. It provides a basis for nuanced discussions about representation of different groups in research, and in clinical drug trials specifically, the implications for such unequal involvement regarding ethics of research. Such a detailed use of demographics can be useful in bringing about a move away from paternalistic practices in medical research.

Clear demographic data can be useful in highlighting exploitative and abusive practices in clinical drug trials. Historically, participants in phase I clinical drug trials were more likely to be vulnerable captive populations (Epstein 2008). Though this changed to voluntary involvement following the passage of the Nuremberg code, the introduction of volunteering brought with it other concerns, such as the exploitation of poor people desperate for money. In addition, the use of the term 'volunteer' suggests such individuals are willing to subject themselves to health risks in order to make a living (Abadie 2010; Fisher 2007). Therefore, having such data helps inform discussion on the demographic characteristics of healthy volunteers in clinical drug trials.

It is widely agreed within bioethics and social science literature that healthy volunteers come from low-income households with low educational attainment, who therefore might be coerced into taking part in clinical drug trials. Tishler and Bartholomae (2002, 2003) research buttresses observations that, in the US at least, poor people are over-represented in clinical drug trials and that most of these tend to be male veteran (repeat) volunteers. However, it is not clear whether this is the case in all countries. It is possible that in other countries or even other states within the US, the picture could be different; that participation in clinical drug trials is not only attractive to ethnic minorities and anarchists groups but might as well appeal to people not so visibly disadvantaged.

The Survey Questionnaire

The discussion in this chapter draws on data derived from a survey questionnaire sent on my behalf to healthy volunteers registered with one CRO in London UK that claims to have more than 80,000 volunteers on its register. The discussion here focuses on demographics such as age, gender, income, and employment. The questionnaire, in addition to providing perceptions of risk and motivation, was also used for recruiting participants for in-depth interviews. In addition, the questionnaire was also important, as it was the first such survey in the UK to be taken among healthy volunteers. Therefore, it provided an overview of possible demographic profiles of healthy volunteers involved in clinical drug trials in the UK.

The limitation of the survey was that it was administered on my behalf by a CRO online to their participants, who may have thought the study was linked to the CRO. Consequently, the sample was nonrandom, and thus the findings might not represent the wider healthy volunteer population involved in healthy volunteer studies because the participants were selected based on their availability. Moreover, only those participants who had access to the Internet could participate in the study. According to the ONS, by 2013 73% of the British adult population accessed the internet every day; 72% of those aged 24–35 were more likely to use the internet, and 67% of the unemployed had used the internet for job applications. It is not clear where they accessed the internet and it is possible that people without internet access who take part in clinical drug trials on a regular basis were omitted from the study. Therefore, it may be difficult to draw wider conclusions about the demographic profile of healthy volunteers. However, from the questionnaire that was sent out electronically, I had 187 healthy volunteer respondents to the survey. Using this sample and the data it generated, it was still possible to conduct an analysis and obtain a meaningful insight into the demographic profiles and attitudes to risk of some healthy volunteers in the UK. It was useful in that it allowed for a comparative analysis of the motivations of healthy volunteers in the UK and substantiated their social context in terms of income, employment, and levels of education.

For the purposes of this discussion, this chapter presents simple descriptive statistics and not detailed or complex statistical analysis. The questionnaire explored healthy volunteers' views of aspects of clinical drug trials and their perceptions of risk. It included questions such as employment status before clinical trial involvement, and employment status at time of completing the questionnaire; type of employment; annual income; number of clinical trials done; if they werer still actively looking to take part in clinical trials; if they would take part in clinical trials for free; and a series of hypothetical questions to assess motivation and risk, among others. This opened up the possibility to explore in greater depth their perceptions and experiences in negotiating risks. Moreover, responses to the questionnaire tended to be positive presentations of selves. Thus, the questionnaire became crucial in informing qualitative interviews.

Findings

Gender and Age Demographics

Of the 187 respondents to the questionnaire, only 122 healthy volunteers responded to the question about their gender. The rationale of the question was to ascertain gender differences in healthy volunteering. Surprisingly 42.6% (52) were male while 57.4% (70) were female, contrary to most research to date, which finds that risk-taking activity such as that associated with clinical drug trials is dominated by males (Byrnes et al. 1999; Gardner and Steinberg 2005). The outcome should be taken with caution as the survey was a self-completed online questionnaire, a type known for attracting more female than male respondents (Sax et al. 2003).

Respondents were asked to state their age, the hypothesis being that young people are more likely to volunteer for clinical drug trials. There were 122 responses, of which 4.9% were aged 18–21, 44.3% were aged 22–29, and the remaining 50.8% (62) were between 30 and 40. None of the respondents indicated they were older than 40.

Contrary to observations that young men are more likely to engage in risk-taking behaviour (Byrnes et al. 1999), respondents in my sample were most likely to be aged 30 or older, followed by those in their late twenties. There were only six 18–21-year-olds. It is also interesting to note that there were more female respondents in this sample than males. The result challenges the view that risk-taking behaviour is the preserve of young men because they are prone to feel invincible, reacting to peer pressure, or searching for the 'buzz' (Gardner and Steinberg 2005). However, clinical drug trials involve different levels of risk, and it is not clear what types of clinical drug trials attract which age and gender categories the most. The type of clinical trial chosen was not asked in the questionnaire but it was raised in subsequent interviews. Nonetheless, though the findings indicate marginal differences in the numbers of female and male involvement in clinical drug trials in the UK, they stand in contrast to US studies by Fisher and Monahan and Fisher, among others, where mostly minority ethnic males are like to be participants. However, as stated earlier, the result should be taken cautiously because of the bias in the sampling technique.

Education

Concerning educational attainment, I set out to investigate if clinical drug trials were, in Schutz's terminology, topically relevant mostly to healthy volunteers with minimal education (secondary school or less). Sixty-five respondents did not answer this question. Of the 122 who responded, 15.6% (19) had GCSE-level education or lower, 37.7% (46) had achieved A-levels, and 46.7% (57) had university degrees or higher qualifications. A chi-square cross-tabulation was conducted to explore a correlation between level of education and willingness to take part in a hypothetical clinical trial if £1000 were offered for a five-night stay, despite potential risks. It found that 74.7% of those with a degree or higher qualification were more likely to express willingness to engage in the hypothetical trial compared to 12.7% of both those with A-levels or equivalent and of those with GCSEs or lower. However, the difference was not statistically significant ($P = 0.375$, $X^2 = 1.960$).

It is interesting that most respondents had attained A-levels or a higher education qualification. Although there may be sample bias, willingness to engage in a hypothetical clinical trial with above-average risks does not seem to be associated with educational attainment. This contradicts assertions that taking part in clinical drug trials are more likely to be attractive to people with low educational attainment. The result also seems to contrast with Monahan and Fisher (2015) study findings, which suggests that in the US, most 'experienced' healthy volunteers, have trade/college or lower-evel education qualification. The findings also counter the view that lack of education leads to risk-taking behaviour in clinical drug trials. The view that lack of education or knowledge may be a good explanation for risk or reckless behaviour underpins most health promotion approaches. It is central to notions of consent in research participation where information provision is seen as empowering individuals to make informed decisions. In Schutz's terminology, information provision to clinical drug trial healthy volunteers aids the interpretational relevance and decision-making process.

Employment: Income and Dependents

To ascertain whether their socioeconomic circumstances were relevant in their decision to take part in clinical drug trials, participants were asked what they did for a living besides volunteering in clinical drug trials. The aim was to see if lack of employment makes taking part in clinical drug trials relevant to some people. Fifty-nine (or 48.4%) of respondents worked full-time, 31.1% (38) worked part-time, and 20.5% (25) were unemployed. Note that the question on employment concerned what the volunteers were doing at the time of the survey as opposed to what they were doing at the time they started taking part in clinical drug trials, a question that was raised in interviews. This was collaborated by professionals who suggested that:

> The (participants are) people who do not have jobs and to some who can fit it among their working days. So some employed people and, um, some people who are technically unemployed...like musicians, actors who...in other words might not have consistent work to go to.... (Professional 2)

To ascertain whether working full-time meant financial security, respondents were asked to state their annual incomes. Eighty-three chose not to state how much they earned annually, but among the remaining 104 respondents, 18.3% (19) earned less than £10,000 a year and 19.2% (20) earned between £11,000 and £15,000. A further 14.4% (15) earned between £16,000 and £20,000, while 48.1% (50) earned more than £21,000 a year. There was no significant correlation between annual income and willingness to take part in a clinical trial if paid £1000. This is not conclusive because there were many nonresponses to the question on income and the sample size was small.

In addition to low income, respondents were also asked to state whether they had dependents at home. The rationale was that people with such responsibilities may find taking part in clinical drug trials attractive because of pressure to provide for their dependents if their incomes were marginal. The data showed that only 10.2% (19) had dependents. The survey found that there was no significant relationship between having dependents and willingness to take part in a clinical trial if paid £1000 lb for a 5-day trial ($x^2 = 2.519$, $P = 0.284$).

The limitations of the sample were that it could have underrepresented the unemployed or people on low incomes and that it was too small compared to the population. Nonetheless, it was surprising that most respondents answering the survey were employed and earned around £20,000 annually, with 48.1% earning more than £21,000. The findings seem to show that in the UK healthy volunteering is not, topically and interpretationally relevant, only to the unemployed or in low income jobs. Rather, it appears that healthy volunteers in the UK may well be earning incomes above the recognised national poverty line, which is defined as less than 60% of the national median income (Padley and Hirsch 2014). It seems that in the UK context, healthy volunteering includes people in diverse financial situations. This presents an interesting image about the relationship between income levels and the cost of living. It would appear that having an income in the range £20,000 or more does not necessarily translate into financial security. As the Joseph

Rowntree Foundation observes, in the recent past there has been an increase in the cost of living in the UK, while wages for most people have remained stagnant.

Therefore, earning what would be considered to be above the poverty line does not necessarily mean people are financially secure. Therefore, this would explain why people who are seemingly earning enough money may resort to clinical trial involvement to supplement their income. In addition, there is also need to consider the complex relationship between finances, social status, and expectations. Though this is often tacit, Western societies have expectations of what one should achieve by a certain age and people are socialised to think that way from an early age. These expectations form the basis for assessing success and establishing status in society. Possessions and lifestyle as indicators of social status and the need to be seen as 'making it' in life all add to the pressure to live up to these expectations. However, as individuals grow, financial inequalities become apparent, particularly when they find themselves in a context of increasing costs of living. In this context, seemingly reasonable income levels become insufficient for sustenance and financial security. This is because it is not possible that a society's cost of living would remain the same; rather, it changes, and sometimes very quickly. Therefore, people in such situations must do whatever it takes to supplement their incomes to live up to the expected or desired social status; this may include taking part in clinical drug trials.

Nationalities and Ethnicities of Healthy Volunteers

Research in the US and New Zealand cited earlier, and even among professional participants in this research, suggests that healthy volunteering is topically and motivationally relevant mostly to ethnic minorities, students (see Monahan and Fisher 2015; Tolich 2010), and unemployed travellers.

> [Previously] a lot of this work was done mostly in students [though] the students have faded away [and been] replaced by…a large part of healthy volunteer[s]…those on one- or two-year working visas coming from the Commonwealth like New Zealand, South Africa and Australia. And…when the eastern European countries joined the EU, we then start to get people from the Baltics. (Professional 2)

Table 4.1 Clinical trial experience of participants

Number of trials done	*Numbers of HVs*
0—Recently registered and actively looking	49
1	69
2–5	37
6–9	8
10—more	13
Would rather not say	12

However, concerning nationality, most respondents to the survey were British citizens (77, or 67.0%), while EU nationals accounted for 18.3% (21), and British residents of non-EU nationalities accounted for 14.8% (17). However, care must be taken when looking at these figures as non-Britons may not have responded to the questionnaire, reducing their representation in the sample, and people with immigration issues could have avoided answering this question or even avoided responding to a questionnaire probing their nationality. Furthermore, the questionnaire was sent out by a CRO. From the responses, indicating thatsome EU nationals take part in clinical drug trials in the UK, it is not clear whether they were resident in the UK at the time of participation or if they come into the UK solely for clinical trial participation purposes. It is possible that cross-border healthy volunteering within the EU takes place, but that was not explicitly shown in the responses. There was also a clear contrast to research from the US cited earlier concerning ethnic representation. Based on this sample, 75.2% participants described themselves as white Caucasian, with Asian Indians making up about 7.7%, and those who described themselves as mixed race making up 5.5%. Black Africans made up about 4.3%. The rest were small percentages of Asian Pakistani, Asian Chinese, and African Caribbean. Likewise, the same practical considerations stated earlier about sampling and generalisability apply here.

Experience

Concerning experience of participating in clinical drug trials, it would appear that from this sample, most participants in clinical drug trials are new participants or those searching to take part in clinical drug trials (see Table 4.1).

While numbers of repeat of volunteers are low, this could be down to two factors. Firstly, it would indicate that the over-volunteering prevention strategy (TOPS) in place is working (Boyce et al. 2012). This is collaborated by accounts by professional views on preventing over volunteering.

> Well, I think TOPS has been very effective in ensuring we do not see repeat volunteers too soon between trials. (Professional 2)

It is possible that TOPS affects how healthy volunteers manage and negotiate their involvement in clinical drug trials. Secondly, the participants' willingness to state exactly how many clinical drug trials they have participated in would have been affected by the fact that the survey was being administered by a CRO; consequently, it is possible that some participants may not have wanted to be identified as over-volunteers.

However, the findings stand in contrast to trends in the US where the majority of healthy volunteers are mostly male ethnic minority serial participants or undocumented migrants (see Fisher 2007; Elliot 2008). Nonetheless, the high numbers of new participants are equally significant as they indicate that healthy volunteering is appealing to a wider audience. It is also, arguably, indicative of a trend that followed events at Northwick Park. According to professional accounts in this research, rather than numbers declining following the tragedy at Northwick Park, professionals talked of an increase in people coming forward to take part in clinical drug trials:

> [After] the [Northwick Park] incident we actually saw an increase in people coming forward to us. So really, no one was put off. Maybe…they [the public] realised there was good money to be earned. (Professional 1)

The reference to financial rewards here is indicative of the problematic relationship between financial rewards, safety, and integrity of clinical drug trials, where payments clearly blinker people's perception of risk. Though the risks associated with taking part in clinical trials may be clear to most people, for some the rewards on offer, obscure risks are involved.

Summary

The survey data and discussion in this chapter has revealed surprising differences in age and income levels, with many university graduates taking part in clinical drug trials in the UK. This is in contrast to findings in research in the US, where healthy volunteers are likely to have college level or lower education. In addition, it seems that in the UK healthy volunteers come from a variety of backgrounds; it is not just the extremely poor who turn to healthy volunteering. In short, the findings ran counter to widely held views of the demographic composition of healthy volunteers. The images of poor and dispossessed people taking part in clinical drug trials did not emerge in the responses to the survey. The findings suggest that, in reality, healthy volunteering is attractive to people from a variety of backgrounds, and my data suggest that reasonable numbers are educated and in employment.

I have to return briefly here to the discussion in Chap. 3 on why a phenomenological approach is important to studying clinical drug trials. Firstly, the diverse nature of participants involved in clinical demonstrates how, if taken for granted, the complex social situations in which individuals or social groups take part in clinical drug trials may remain understood as normal and therefore acceptable. Secondly, the findings suggest that healthy volunteering is also closely linked to the material conditions in which people find themselves. To that end, motivations for healthy volunteering should equally be seen in the context of the neoliberal agenda that shifts the state's responsibility for welfare to the individual citizen. This shift in responsibility coupled with poor socioeconomic circumstances creates a situation where taking part in clinical drug trials becomes a viable option for some people in society. In addition, the findings illustrate how healthy volunteering could derive from a desire to make a living or live up to expected social standards. This is because the social environments are responsible for producing meanings and definitions of liveable lifestyles. The lack of those material conditions and resources deemed necessary for such a life in some circumstances lead some to become guinea pigs (Abadie 2010; Elliot 2008).

The findings in this chapter provide an opportunity to reassess understandings of ethics and justice in relation to people seen as vulnerable subjects in medical research and views about healthy volunteering in general. Specifically, though I have pointed out that high living costs and social expectations may pressure people into healthy volunteering, the findings provide a platform for exploring further why people who may be described as having an annual income well above poverty line find taking part in clinical drug trials an attractive endeavour. In the following section, I discuss motivations for people's involvement in clinical drug trials using interview data to elaborate on the findings from the sample survey.

References

Abadie, R. (2010). *The professional guinea pig: Big pharma and the risky world of human subjects*. London: Duke University Press.

Boyce, M., et al. (2012). TOPS: An internet-based system to prevent healthy subjects from over-volunteering for clinical drug trials. *European Journal of Clinical Pharmacology, 68*(7), 1019–1024.

Byrnes, J. P., et al. (1999). Gender differences in risk taking: A meta-analysis. *Psychological Bulletin, 125*(3), 367.

Elliott, C. (2008). Guinea-pigging: Healthy human subjects for drug safety trials are in demand. But is it a living?. New Yorker (New York).

Epstein, S. (2008). The rise of recruitmentology: Clinical research, racial knowledge, and the politics of inclusion and difference. *Social Studies of Science, 38*(5), 801–832.

Fisher, J. A. (2007). Coming soon to a physician near you: Medical neoliberalism and pharmaceutical clinical drug trials. *Harvard Health Policy Review: A Student Publication of the Harvard Interfaculty Initiative in Health Policy, 8*(1), 61.

Frank, G. (2004). Current challenges in clinical trial patient recruitment and enrollment. *SoCRA Source, 30*. Available at: http://www.socra.org/pdf/200402_Current_Challenges_Recruitment_Enrollment.pdf.

Gardner, M., & Steinberg, L. (2005). Peer influence on risk taking, risk preference, and risky decision making in adolescence and adulthood: An experimental study. *Developmental Psychology, 41*(4), 625.

Monahan, T., & Fisher, J. A. (2015). "I'm still a Hustler": Creative and entrepreneurial responses to precarity by participants in phase I clinical drug trials. *Economy and Society, 44*, 545–566.

Padley, M., & Hirsch, D. (2014). *Households below a minimum income standard: 2008/2009 to 2011/2012*. Joseph Rowntree Foundation. Available at: http://www.jrf.org.uk/publications/households-below-minimum-income-standard.

Sax, L. J., Gilmartin, S. K., & Bryant, A. N. (2003). Assessing response rates and nonresponse bias in web and paper surveys. *Research in Higher Education, 44*(4), 409–432.

Tishler, C. L., & Bartholomae, S. (2002). The recruitment of normal healthy volunteers: A review of the literature on the use of financial incentives. *The Journal of Clinical Pharmacology, 42*(4), 365–375.

Tishler, C. L., & Bartholomae, S. (2003). Repeat participation among normal healthy research volunteers: Professional guinea pigs in clinical trials? *Perspectives in Biology and Medicine, 46*(4), 508–520.

Tolich, M. (2010). What if Institutional Review Boards (IRBs) treated healthy volunteers in clinical trials as their clients?. *Australasian Medical Journal, 3*(12).

CHAPTER 5

'Context Is Everything': The Reality of Becoming a Human Guinea Pig

Abstract This chapter focuses on people's motivation for becoming involved in healthy volunteering. I show how healthy volunteers start their volunteering journeys and question assumptions of healthy volunteers as 'risky' and 'reckless' individuals. The discussion considers why financial rewards in clinical drug trials become significant to some people who take part in clinical drug trials as healthy volunteers. In exploring motivations of healthy volunteers, I challenge the principle of voluntarism by considering how socioeconomic circumstances play a role in influencing people to healthy volunteers.

Keywords Motivations · Debt · Volunteering · Volunteers · Clinical drug trials · Financial rewards

Healthy Volunteer Motivations

Most medical research on healthy volunteering emphasises altruism and the desire to learn more about therapies as major motivating factors for volunteers (Truong et al. 2011). One study showed that access to health benefits during a trial was an important incentive for cancer patients (Nurgat et al. 2005). However, motivations for healthy volunteers are different from those of patients. Social scientists who have explored motivations for participation in clinical drug trials generally agree that monetary rewards are the major motivating factors for healthy volunteers. A mixed methods Brazilian study found that the most frequently

S. Mwale, *Healthy Volunteers in Commercial Clinical Drug Trials*,
DOI 10.1007/978-3-319-59214-5_5

cited reasons for involvement in clinical drug trials were monetary rewards and access to healthcare (Nappo et al. 2013). Similarly, research cited earlier in this book (Abadie 2010; Tishler and Bartholomae 2002; Tolic) points to financial rewards as motivations for healthy volunteer involvement in clinical drug trials in the US and New Zealand and illustrates the need for exploring the wider context in which such acts take place. In addition to financial rewards, US research suggests healthy volunteers are also motivated by the need to access healthcare too (see Fisher 2007). In the UK, healthcare is free at the point of delivery. Therefore, understanding healthy volunteer motivations requires considering the wider socioeconomic and political contexts.

While emerging research in the US (Abadie 2010; Elliott 2014; Trisher and Bartholomae 2002; Fisher 2007 among others) is encouraging, the extant research has been US-centred with little focus in other parts of the world, including the UK, on the phenomenon of healthy volunteering. Where this has been attempted in the UK, there has been little focus on why financial rewards become relevant motivations for some healthy volunteers. In other words, questions about why monetary rewards are attractive to certain individuals are often unexplored in the UK. In addition, most research in the UK has examined why patients rather than healthy volunteers seek to take part in clinical drug trials (Featherstone 2003; Morris and Bàlmer 2006). While this is useful, the motivations for healthy volunteer participation, which may potentially be altruistic as well, are very different from those of patients as they have no health benefits to gain, save for free health checks.

To illustrate the complexity of understand healthy volunteer motivations, I outline how life events interact with sociopolitical and socioeconomic circumstances to make healthy volunteering of a viable option for some people people's decisions. By life events, I mean adverse circumstances such as job loss and increasing debt, and their relevance in influencing individuals to become healthy volunteers in clinical drug trials.

As established in the previous chapter, contrary to trends in the US, the survey showed that healthy volunteering is not attractive only to the unemployed and the marginalised, but that in the UK context it also attracts those who are well-educated and holding relatively well-paid jobs. The evidence illustrates the complicated nature of the relationship between financial incentives and social circumstances. The difficult financial circumstances healthy volunteers find themselves in can be compared to people who are in financial debt. Research suggests that people who are in debt take desperate measures, borrowing more money and getting deeper into debt (Montgomerie and Williams 2009). The same could be said of people who take part in clinical drug trials. In times of an economic downturn, many have lost their jobs and livelihoods and alternative employment may be hard to come by. Some believe they have no choice but to volunteer for clinical drug trials. This shows how people in precarious financial situations may take desperate actions to address their financial problems.

Monetary Reward as Motivation

It is important that the question of financial rewards is addressed from the outset. In the research informing the discussion in this book and from the literature (Stunkel and Grady 2011; Tishler and Bartholomae 2002), it is clear that for most respondents, financial rewards on offer are their primary motivation for getting into healthy volunteering. Most participants in this research also acknowledged this fact.

> The money is very important. If they put something in my body, they have to pay me. (Jon, male, 31)

> Obviously for me it's about the money. That's why I am doing it. (Sasha, female, 27)

Equally professionals working in the CRO industry confirmed this to be the case, as the following extract shows.

> Well, it is obvious that these individuals get involved in our studies because of the money that is on offer. That is mainly the reason. (CRO Professional 1)

This is supported by findings from the questionnaires. The respondents were asked to consider a series of hypothetical questions. When asked how strongly they agreed or disagreed with the statement 'Monetary compensation was important in my decision to take part in clinical drug trials', 51.2% (62) agreed and 38.0% (46) strongly agreed with the statement compared to 0.8% (1) and 4.1% (5) disagreeing and strongly disagreeing, respectively. The respondents were also asked how extremely likely or extremely unlikely they were to take part in clinical drug trials if there was no monetary reward. Most of the respondents were not willing to take part in clinical drug trials if payments were not included.

52.8% (66) stated that it was extremely unlikely and 23.2% (29) said that it was unlikely compared to 1.6% (2) and 4.8% (6) who stated they were extremely likely and likely, respectively, to take part without payment. The remaining 17.6% (22) were unsure. Of additional significance was the fact that, even higher-income respondents acknowledged monetary reward to be a strong motivation.

Most discussions about motivation for volunteering in clinical drug trials stop at this point, acknowledging that people are motivated by financial rewards but then emphasise altruism and other reasons such as access to healthcare and fascination with science, for instance. As Fisher (2007) observes, there is a tendency to see volunteers as willing and altruistic individuals. Such views of willing subjects are in keeping with the concept of individuals as rational actors, as discussed in Chap. 2. A problem with such a view is that it results in a smooth narrative of motivations, negating the contexts and circumstances of people's lives and their relevance for people's motivations to become healthy volunteers. Relationships between money, the body, and risk-taking are complex and often contradictory; decisions to take part in clinical drug trials often involve a consideration of several issues or what in Schutz terminology is a 'system of relevances' (Schutz 1970) rather than a simple utilitarian cost-benefit analysis. As one professional from one CRO explained:

> I think … that money has different significance to people who are in different life situations. So if you are struggling…um, or let's say if you come from Poland, a small amount of money in this country, if you send it back to Poland…uh…can buy a lot more, and similarly for other eastern European countries, maybe South America, too. So there is more of an inducement for people in certain situations. (CRO Professional 1)

Understanding motivations for healthy volunteering in commercial phase 1 drug trials requires looking beyond the signed consent form to explore wider issues that can otherwise be taken for granted (Back 2015; Schutz 1970). This involves presenting both the contradictions and similarities in people's explanations for motivations. In the following section, I consider how different factors shape people's motivation for involvement in clinical drug trials.

Becoming a Healthy Volunteer

The participants in the research seemed to have different life experiences that led them to consider taking part in clinical drug trials. For the majority of the participants, the main issue was being in a situation best described as some kind of financial crisis. This crisis can be categorised further into debt, unemployment, and insufficient income.

Personal Debt Crises

For most of the respondents in this project, volunteering in clinical drug trials was not something they wanted to do. Rather, it became topically relevant because they considered their financial situations to be beyond their control:

> I was in some debt that really needed to be paid off, otherwise I was going to be in some shit if I didn't, you know. So it was kind of a situation where I had to do that to get myself out of the sticky situation I was in. (Sam, male, 30)

> I was ... just out of a job at the time, and I needed a little bit more extra cash obviously to survive and it was a good way to make, a quick way to make big sum of money, and yeah [laughs] to pay off debts. (Jayne, female, 26)

> I had bills and some debts to settle... if I didn't do anything this was going to be a really shit situation with bailiffs knocking on my door. (Chase, male, 33)

For these participants, debts and bills were the precursor of their involvement in clinical drug trials. One would ask: why clinical drug trials? However, before becoming involved in clinical drug trials, most participants talked of trying out other options, such as finding a job. In Schutz's terminology, this would be called interpretive relevance. Finding a job either failed to solve the problem, or there was no job to be had. It was at this point that clinical drug trials became motivationally relevant.

Unemployment and Intermittent Work

While for some, debts were an issue, for other participants taking part in clinical drug trials was relevant because they were at the time unemployed or did not have permanent jobs that would have guaranteed a steady income. For these participants, being unemployed or having unsteady income made them think of doing something about their situation:

> When I started, I mean did my first trial, I had no job and it was kind of hard, kind of fed-up being supported by my mum. (Jayne, female, 26)

> I had been for a while out of a job and so I needed to do something to get by doing a trial to get by. (Jon, male, 31)

For some participants in temporary employment, this meant that their source of income was uncertain. Therefore, taking part in clinical drug trials helped them to get by while waiting for job offers. For instance, Lucy had a job, but spoke of the temporary nature of jobs such as modelling and acting, which involve short-term contracts:

> I do clinical drug trials when I am not on set to supplement my income. As you may know, work in my field can be erratic… I tried other temping jobs but it was going to take too long to get them paid off. (Lucy, female, 25)

What is important in these accounts is how people in a precarious situation felt they had to make decisions to resolve what they felt were pressing financial situations. These were not attempts to get rich, but actions aimed at providing for themselves to survive.

Employed but Insufficient Income

Some of the participants who reported having a job also talked of being in a financial crisis of some sort. These participants believed that their earnings would not resolve their problems such as debt, suggesting it would take a long time to pay off the debt. For others taking part in clinical drug trials supplemented their daily living costs.

> I would never have managed to pay off the debt if I had relied on the job so the only way was taking part in a trial…At the time the pay was not enough for me to cover for that. (Matt, male, 28)

> At the time (I started taking part in clinical drug trials), I had a job, the pay was good and everything...but I had some debt that needed urgently (paying) off. I could not have managed to pay off the debt if I had relied on the job so the only way was taking part in a trial. (Ed, male, 28)

Of interest in these accounts is the participants' feelings that their pay would not be sufficient to resolve their problems. This illustrates the complexity of the relationship between income and cost of living. While common assumptions are that individuals in well-paid work may not take part in such risky activities, insufficient incomes make them consider alternative ways to make a living. It is worth noting how participants used accounts of their social circumstances as topical and motivational relevance for taking part in clinical drug trials; their decisions seem intended to deflect criticism for what others might see as risky behaviour:

> That time (when I took part in the first trial) I was unemployed and was, well, let's say I was struggling financially and I didn't have much of a choice but to volunteer in clinical drug trials because I badly needed some money to pay bills, rent, etc. I also had credit card bills to settle....I looked for normal jobs but couldn't find any. (Jon, male, 31)

Of interest here, is the participants' feelings of having 'no choice' but to engage in healthy volunteering. By evoking the idea of not having a choice, it would appear that the participants seemed to be justifying their decisions to take part in clinical drug trials.

How Did They Hear About Clinical Drug Trials?

If taking part in clinical drug trials was a response to a financial crisis, it begs the question, how did they come to think of healthy volunteering as a solution? The participants gave different accounts. Some talked of hearing about clinical drug trials through media advertisements or after friends had told them how much money they had earned healthy volunteering.

> At the time my friend was doing this. He told me about clinical trials and how much money you can make in a short time, such kind of thing, and then I registered. (Joe, male, 29)

> Well, my boyfriend started first, so he told me about it [pause] and [pause] told me that it was safe and that it was a good thing to do...[I] thought it

> was an opportunity to help other people [winks] and make some money at the same time [laughs out loud at the mention of money]...yeah! (Melisa, female, 24)

The participants who had heard about clinical drug trials from friends or relatives talked of how easy it was to decide to volunteer. For them the trust they had in the individual who was encouraging them was crucial. Such participants seemed to have little problem deciding to register as they had the assurance of someone they trusted who was not a medical professional. It is interesting to observe here how lay accounts and experiences of health and risk can influence decisions and behaviour.

For others, it was advertisements or media reporting that made healthy volunteering of interest. The Northwick Park incident aroused widespread interest for some participants who noted how much reward had been offered to volunteers in the trial.

> To start with, I got interested in trials after that one that went really badly wrong [Northwick Park]. It got me thinking so I started to look out for more trials. This one they actually contacted me. There are a number of websites such as trials4us.co.uk...you fill out, like, a basic application. (Colin, male, 26)

Note the significance of relationships in shaping risk decision-making in the quotes. The people my participants interacted with were very useful in helping them get started in taking part in clinical drug trials. Strangely, disasters that would put others off seemed to make some more interested.

Clinical Drug Trials Involvement as a Pragmatic Measure

In general, the preceding discussion illustrates how personal financial crises and circumstances coupled with the monetary rewards on offer made taking part in clinical drug trials a relevant course of action for some healthy volunteers. However, before turning to clinical drug trials, participants talked of considering other options to resolve their financial problems, which upon interpretation made monetary rewards in clinical drug trials a motivational relevance (Schutz 1970). The financial situation of some respondents was so serious that they felt they were 'between a rock and a hard place'. Nevertheless, the decision to become a healthy volunteer was not easily taken.

> So it was a must-do-something situation for me because I couldn't bear the thought of what was coming if I hadn't done something at that time. Not that the decision was easy to do this – both options were hard. It was like bite the bullet and live, or fall of the cliff or face the hungry beasts, that bad...you know, but like a short stop-gap. (Conor, male, 32)

> Of course I considered looking for another job or something...if I worked it would have had to be a pretty good job if I was going to pay off the debt but I couldn't get find such a job. (Jaque, female, 25)

These quotes illustrate how desperate the situation had become for the participants, leading them to healthy volunteering albeit as a temporal measure. Most participants did not intend to make taking part in clinical drug trials a regular practice; it was rather an impromptu response to a situation thought to be running out of control.

> Oh yes, I did not have the job at the time...So I got into this [volunteering] you know, as a sort of, um, one-off solution, um, like last resort but not to be done again, that kind of thing. (Jodie, female, 26)

> I did not intend to do a trial after that, though ... It was intended to be a one-off thing, pay the debt and move on to normal life. (Matt, male, 28)

Here I have to take us back to Asha's account outlined in the first chapter. Asha, an immigrant, was forced by her then-boyfriend to participate in clinical drug trials against her will. The earlier quotes and Asha's story demonstrate the significance of the shared sense of having 'no other option'. It seems whether coerced by someone or by social circumstances, participants in this research felt that taking part in clinical drug trials was the only way out of their problems.

The discussion here shows how periods of unemployment, unpaid bills, and rising debt can combine to make taking part in clinical drug trials topically, interpretively, and motivationally relevant (Schutz 1970), for some even when they subsequently have paid work. The situations the participants found themselves explain why certain groups of people take part in clinical drug trials. Looking at healthy volunteering in this way, challenges the view of healthy volunteers as 'willing' and 'ready to recruit' (Fisher 2007) and shows how their financial vulnerability leads them to healthy volunteering.

Overall, the participants seemed to take a 'pragmatic' approach in response to problems they felt needed addressing urgently. Failure to do so, at least for them, would have brought problems such as the shame of facing court bailiffs. These individuals had to do something to avoid the consequences of continued financial problems that seemed to be spiralling out of control.

Health Crisis in the Family and Heath Checks as Motivation

For some participants, taking part in clinical drug trials was prompted not only by their financial problems but also by setbacks in other areas of their lives, such as the declining health of a family member. Such crises seemed to intensify the realisation of their own fragility. Becoming a healthy volunteer was a solution: in addition to earning money, they would be medically examined, increasing the chance of early detection of a serious illness. Their motivations were less altruistic than personal, and even selfish. Asked if they would take part in a clinical trial for free if invited, one replied:

> I think my dad had just been diagnosed with late onset diabetes which really affected him badly, so I was starting to think more about my own health and worrying about things that I did not know about my health that could be, you know, going haywire. So I thought doing such things would provide an opportunity for them to do a test, like an MoT [Ministry of Transport check for roadworthiness] like on your body. (Innocent, male, 24)

Of course, one could always go to a GP for a check-up, but some respondents thought that GPs would not have enough time to examine someone without an obvious illness. They preferred clinical drug trials to accessing primary care because they felt that the nature of encounters with the GPs meant that they could not be thorough enough or have the time to see them if they did not have any physical illness. Healthy volunteers Bob and Matt shared their views of medical check-ups:

> Like a car MOT, you know [you] can get that from your GP but it's something you have to push for. Besides, I don't think they [GPs] can do it as often as I would like to have it done for obvious reasons, you know, time and budgets. You also get a sense of rushing when you are talking to GPs but in units (clinical drug trials wards) on a trial, it's more thorough. (Bob, male, 25)

> I rarely visit the GP, so I suppose this 'screen' acts as my check-up. Not sure if that makes sense. Because GPs are generally slow and the procedure is just cumbersome…but on the clinical trial it's thorough and quick. (Matt, male, 28)

> So I kind of get [my health] check but also contribute to helping someone at the same time if the drug is developed kind of thing. (Chase, male, 33)

For one participant, the decision to take part in clinical drug trials came about after a family member wanted a child but was struggling to conceive. This made the informant think about health issues in a broader sense:

> I guess partly the reason I started doing the studies that I am doing now is that it was about a fertility study…at the time my brother was having his first child after some struggles so I was kind of attuned to it a bit more. (Jayne, female, 26)

This discussion illustrates that although people appreciated the reward on offer in clinical drug trials, some were also willing to do clinical drug trials for some kind of health benefit. For these people becoming a guinea pig was a way of dealing with uncertainties about their health. For others the trial was a way of checking on their health along the lines of a body 'MOT', drawing comparisons to tests carried out on cars to check for roadworthiness. The family problems included, among others, health problems of genetic origin or those that might arise if they did not check their health status regularly. For some participants, health issues experienced by other family member were a motivational relevance. Analysis of the accounts in this section shows that participants saw taking part in clinical drug trials as a way of avoiding risk rather than taking additional risks. Also of interest is how the accounts seemed to be used as a careful way of claiming altruism, as could be seen in the last quote. This is interesting as participants felt that this was a justifiable way of engaging with risk.

Biographical Situation

As in the preceding section, for a minority of participants, in addition to financial rewards, their biographical situations also had motivational relevance for getting involved in clinical drug trials. In using 'biographical situation', I refer to Schutz's analysis of how one's socialisation provides the basis for beliefs, views, and knowledge of the world around oneself. For some respondents, taking part in clinical drug trials was an opportunity to act on their beliefs, as expressed in the quote below:

> I do clinical drug trials because I do not believe in animal testing, so you know, you can't be against something if you cannot come forward and do something about it. So I am interested because I want to do my bit in stopping animal testing. Animals should not be used to solve our own problems that we bring on ourselves. (Lucy, female, 25)

This is a different expression of altruism, one of 'doing one's part' to develop safe, effective drugs while protecting animals. Another volunteer was motivated to take part in clinical drug trials to achieve certain personal goals and to use the opportunity to build contacts, particularly with medical researchers, in a chosen field of work. Others chose to participate because of their interest in the role and function of medicines in the developing world:

> So yeah, it's not just about the money…well, I do need the money badly, obviously…I want to work in clinical drug trials in the future so I hope to build contacts but I feel someone has to help others and at this time I feel it's my turn to do that [volunteer in the clinical trial]. (Hope, female, 34)

> It's not for the money only [laughs]…it's also about helping others to some degree. Medicines are needed everywhere in the world to help the sick so I play that small part in a way. (Lucy, female, 25)

Some of these accounts are noteworthy for the undertone of self-justification. The respondents did not want to be stereotyped as lazy and reckless individuals, but rather as reasonable people with varied interests and aims or even as selfless. Most of the interviews were done in public spaces and possibly the participants would have wanted to be seen in a positive light, especially when being asked questions by a stranger (Callon and Rabeharisoa 2004; Will and Weiner 2014). Others rejected the idea that they had to justify themselves in any way. They stated clearly that their involvement in clinical drug trials was purely for the money.

> I do this and others do it purely for money and if anyone says otherwise I disagree, it's bullshit excuses. People do this for money, not to help science or develop medicine...I actually find it annoying when people talk to me about my volunteering in medical trials and make me feel like I am a lazy, selfish person...it is hard work doing clinical drug trials. (Sam, male, 30)

Of interest, here is how Sam questions normative assumptions about 'normal' ways of earning money. From another perspective, healthy volunteering can constitute resistance to social expectations as people get involved in what is normally seen as a risky and even reckless venture. In so doing they challenge these social expectations of acceptable ways of earning a living. This is an aspect of the 'moral economy' (Scott 1977) and positive public views of risk-taking (Lyng 2009) that relates to the desperate nature of volunteers' social situations and circumstances—their conception of work and social justice, what it takes to survive in a market economy, and how these factors interact to drive them to risk their health. To understand better why people turn to healthy volunteering requires accepting, first, that their decisions are dictated by the need for survival. Then one should the interactions between the state, professionals, and corporations on one hand, and family and society on the other. Doing so reveals the relevance of these interactions in driving individuals into the risky business of healthy volunteering. Obviously, this means reframing a range of issues, notably meanings of financial security, meaning of volunteering, and rational consent as outlined in the opening chapters of this book.

In addition, Scott's concept of 'moral economy' can be applied to people—individually and not collectively—who decide to volunteer for clinical drug trials. The healthy volunteers in this research held strong beliefs about the right to have enough to survive as independent individuals. They also wanted to live up to social standards of acceptability and to avoid the shame associated with failing to earn enough. They also initially demonstrated an antipathy to the risks (Peretti-Watel and Moatti 2006) inherent in participating in clinical drug trials. For most of the respondents, the goal was not to become rich but rather to avoid the problem of unemployment and the shame of being unable to support themselves (and possibly their families). Therefore, to construe healthy volunteers as aspiring to become rich or lazy fails to appreciate the reality of everyday dilemmas in their quest for survival in a market economy.

Scott (1977) shifts resistance from the periphery, where it is likely to be viewed as the actions of a few disgruntled individuals, to the ways in which society produces certain forms of agency. In this case, inequality leads individuals to engage in activities often frowned upon in order to make a living. The discussion in this chapter on the reality of financial circumstances of healthy volunteers reflects the nature of the market economy, which flourishes amid the widening gap in incomes and increasing social inequality (Stiglitz 2012). Increasing unemployment among graduates means that many approach their 30s with inadequate incomes and without a job. The high cost of living in London, where most of the participants in this research were from, could also qualify what a 'reasonable' income might mean for different people.

Summary

This chapter has looked at the reality surrounding healthy volunteer involvement in clinical drug trials. The discussion highlights the significance of considering the wider context in which acts of volunteering takes place. To incessant advocates of rationality and individual liberty in a neoliberal context, healthy volunteers are a population of willing participants and entrepreneurs looking for competitive unregulated space in a free market. However, it only makes sense to see these people as financially straitened individuals whose personal circumstances drive them to healthy volunteering for subsistence and inadvertently become a readily available exploitable resource in clinical drug trials. Clearly, healthy volunteers' actions are driven by the need to survive, challenging assumptions that healthy volunteers are looking for easy money or are not interested in finding a normal job. It is clear from accounts cited in this chapter that monetary rewards are the major motivation for getting involved in clinical drug trials, and their motivations are complicated. The respondents acknowledge that they had volunteered mainly to address their financial problems; they had failed to find other solutions and believed that their only option was to take part in clinical drug trials. Some, in addition to financial rewards, seemed keen to justify their actions by giving other reasons for having participated in the trials. Not wishing to be seen as reckless, the participants generally reject the notion that they had 'volunteered'.

I argue that healthy volunteering is a means of survival for most participants, and that conceptions of vulnerability in legal and regulatory discourses should be broadened to include people who may be financially disadvantaged. This is because regulation and ethics play a role in defining and legitimising certain forms of agency. The chapter has also shown how institutional contexts of personal debt, rising costs of living, and unemployment act as topical and motivational relevance, leading some individuals into healthy volunteering. The participants in this research talked of looking for conventional means such as a job to resolve their financial problems (interpretational relevance), before turning to healthy volunteering. In addition, looking for other options before taking to healthy volunteering is in keeping with what Bloor (1995) calls the polythetic nature of decision-making in which individuals explore various possible options available in search for appropriate response to social stimuli. Furthermore, the participants' accounts of unemployment and debt (among other reasons) as precursors to healthy volunteering illustrates how relevances may be imposed by wider sociopolitical and socioeconomic contexts. Using this framework shows how a better understanding healthy of volunteering, their motivations, and conceptions of risk requires looking beyond the utilitarian ethics of rationality, choice, and cost-benefit analysis to consider how increasing inequality plays out to driving people to desperate actions in order to survive.

References

Abadie, R. (2010). *The professional guinea pig: Big pharma and the risky world of human subjects*. London: Duke University Press.

Back, L. (2015). Why everyday life matters: Class, community and making life livable. *Sociology, 49*(5), 820–836.

Bloor, M. (1995). *The sociology of HIV transmission*. London: Sage.

Callon, M., & Rabeharisoa, V. (2004). Gino's lesson on humanity: Genetics, mutual entanglements and the sociologist's role. *Economy and Society, 33*(1), 1–27.

Elliott, C. (2014, July 28). The best-selling, billion-dollar pills tested on homeless people: How the destitute and the mentally ill are being used as human lab rats. *Medium*. https://medium.com/matter/did-big-pharma-test-your-meds-on-homeless-people-a6d8d3fc7dfe.

Featherstone, K. (2003). The experience of trial participation [Editorial]. *The Journal of Rheumatology, 30*(4), 646–647.

Fisher, J. A. (2007). Coming soon to a physician near you: Medical neoliberalism and pharmaceutical clinical drug trials. *Harvard Health Policy Review: A Student Publication of the Harvard Interfaculty Initiative in Health Policy, 8*(1), 61.

Lyng, S. (2009 [2008]). Edgework, risk, and uncertainty. In J. Zinn (Ed.), *Social theories of risk and uncertainty: An introduction* (pp. 106–135). Oxford: Blackwell Publishers.

Montgomerie, J., & Williams, K. (2009). Financialised capitalism: After the crisis and beyond neoliberalism. *Competition & Change, 13*(2), 99–107.

Morris, N., & Bàlmer, B. (2006). Volunteer human subjects' understandings of their participation in a biomedical research experiment. *Social Science and Medicine, 62*(4), 998–1008.

Nappo, S. A., Iafrate, G. B., & Sanchez, Z. M. (2013). Motives for participating in a clinical research trial: A pilot study in Brazil. *BMC Public Health, 13*(1), 19.

Nurgat, Z. A., et al. (2005). Patient motivations surrounding participation in phase I and phase II clinical drug trials of cancer chemotherapy. *British Journal of Cancer, 92*(6), 1001–1005.

Peretti-Watel, P., & Moatti, J. (2006). Understanding risk behaviours: How the sociology of deviance may contribute? The case of drug-taking. *Social Science and Medicine, 63*(3), 675–679.

Schutz, A. (1970). *Reflections on the problem of relevance* (R. M. Zaner, Trans.). New Haven: Yale University Press.

Scott, J. C. (1977). *The moral economy of the peasant: Rebellion and subsistence in Southeast Asia*. New Haven: Yale University Press.

Stiglitz, J. E. (2012). *The price of inequality: How today's divided society endangers our future*. New York: W. W. Norton.

Stunkel, L., & Grady, C. (2011). More than the money: A review of the literature examining healthy volunteer motivations. *Contemporary Clinical Drug Trials, 32*(3), 342–352.

Tishler, C. L., & Bartholomae, S. (2002). The recruitment of normal healthy volunteers: A review of the literature on the use of financial incentives. *The Journal of Clinical Pharmacology, 42*(4), 365–375.

Truong, T. H., et al. (2011). Altruism among participants in cancer clinical drug trials. *Clinical Drug Trials (London, England), 8*(5): 616–623.

Will, C. M., & Weiner, K. (2014). Sustained multiplicity in everyday cholesterol reduction: Repertoires and practices in talk about "healthy living". *Sociology of Health & Illness, 36*(2), 291–304.

CHAPTER 6

Economic Exchanges? Healthy Volunteering as a Form of Labour

Abstract While the previous two chapters question the idea of autonomy in healthy volunteering, here I interrogate the notion and discourse of altruism that permeates discussions of healthy volunteering in clinical drug trials. Drawing on accounts of healthy volunteers' experiences in clinical drug trials, this chapter challenges the tendency to situate healthy volunteers as willing and altruistic in their actions. I argue that healthy volunteering is infact a form of economic exchange in which the body is exchanged for the financial rewards on offer and it is in fact a form of passive labour. The history of healthy volunteering as an exchange can be traced to post-war changes in the regulation, organisation, and practice of clinical drug trials, which led to the birth and subsequent growth of CROs. Today, CROs pride themselves at being effective and efficient in recruiting the right kind of trial participants and being competent in managing studies. Consequently, recruitment of participants has become a lucrative business for the CROs. The increasing numbers of CROs have intensified competition in the national and global search for healthy volunteers and has resulted in an increase in amounts of monetary rewards offered to healthy volunteers for participating in clinical drug trials.

Keywords Exchange · Healthy volunteers · Clinical drug trials · Body Power · Labour · Financial rewards

S. Mwale, *Healthy Volunteers in Commercial Clinical Drug Trials*,
DOI 10.1007/978-3-319-59214-5_6

Total Institution: Becoming 'Valuable Data'

A 'total institution' resembles a totalitarian social system in which the whole being of the individual is completely absorbed by the system in which they live (Goffman 1961). In this context, individuals are subject to a rigid way of life and with little or no space for the individual's desires, aspirations, and individuality. Organised in this way, individuals cannot escape and their dignity is ignored. Participants in this study spoke of noticing a change in attitude on the part of the research teams once they were admitted into the trials. They experienced a sense of being depersonalised and institutionalised, in an echo of Goffman's concept of 'total institution'. Being recruited for a clinical trial is easy, as outlined in Chap. 1: on receiving or seeing an advertisement, one simply enters details online to express an interest in an advertised trial, and then waiting to be called for an assessment. The assessment confirms whether the individual fits the requirements of the study in terms of height, weight, and other vital signs. It is upon admission into the trial that participants' talked of what most referred to as 'becoming data'. By this, they were referring to the changes in how they were treated pre- and post-admission into the clinical drug trial. This process is linked closely to the sense of becoming depersonalised and institutionalised.

Depersonalisation and Institutionalisation

Depersonalisation refers to a loss of subjective identity which results in a feeling that one is reduced to being a mere component in a system (Goffman 1961). This experience of depersonalisation could arguably be linked to what Cooper and Waldby (2014) call clinical labour, in which human involvement in medical research is seen as part of the creation of biovalue (Mitchell and Waldby 2010) in emerging bio-economies. Biovalue broadly refers to how life and profits are derived from exploiting the living process of the human body and its components using medico-technological innovations. Arguably, the depersonalisation experienced by healthy volunteers is characteristic of clinical labour as their bodies are seen primarily in terms of their potential for profit in bio-economies. Most participants described their experiences during clinical drug trials as dehumanising.

> The other issue with trials is that...once you enrol, you become just a number; you are just there, you are not you...it can be quite hard to deal with sometimes, and the powerlessness as well...because basically to them you are just data, you know, but have value in the form of data and the money it represents, not the human being I am. (Jazza, male, 28)

Some participant's spoke of 'becoming a number' or 'becoming just data' and feeling a loss of identity; while others talked of feeling like guinea pigs:

> I also felt much like a laboratory rat, like a testing animal, especially when you are not treated well by the nurses...Sometimes you are treated like a number on their sheets and not a person. (Jon, male 31)

> To them we were just numbers on hospital beds and not people. It's quite strange, not that it was obvious, but in subtle ways. But you know, it does really feel that you are just a specimen on the trial. (Lucy, female, 25)

> Yes, I felt abused, like I am a secondary human being. Like, ah, like, um, not even a human being, like a lab rat....this made you feel unequal.]...I felt really, like, insane, like quite mad. (Jodie, female, 26)

The depersonalised nature of such experiences is significant in two ways. Firstly, for the participants this demonstrated the economic nature of healthy volunteering and how healthy volunteers become commodities. Volunteers felt that they no longer had control over what happened to them and realised that their feelings were not be taken into account. Secondly, they experienced a loss of power and control and felt like unequal objects, their humanity unacknowledged. The research team controlled their movements, diets, and food intake, and also contact with the outside world. The participants had a rigorous schedule detailing every procedure, minute by minute, which added to feelings of powerlessness and the challenge of enduring procedures they were subjected to. However, not everyone experienced negative feelings. Asked what it felt like being on a clinical drug trial some participants said:

> I am fascinated by medical research...but...you must go in ready to deal with that mentally...also be ready to cope with the food because it's not pleasant food. So go in ready to eat shit food. (Ed, male, 28)

> I go into trial ready to deal with whatever comes so I don't feel used at all and I don't mind those who try to boss or their rules, because I go in mentally ready…and it does not bother me…I mean the research team or their rules. I am also captivated by science, so that gives me a chance to see it close by. (Rob, male, 28)

These two participants were evidently so intrigued by the processes involved in the clinical trial that they came prepared mentally for the experience such that the power dynamics were of relatively little concern.

As mentioned earlier, institutionalisation refers to ways in which individual behaviours and actions are defined and limited by an institution. While a small section of the participants found relationships during the trial to be cordial, each day was structured strictly around fixed rules. Therefore, in addition to being depersonalised, and perhaps as part of the depersonalisation process, they were subject to in-house rules that were non-negotiable. The participants felt that by this time they had been reduced to being a small yet valuable part of the clinical trial process.

> They are just interested in my body and the results that my body will give them. After which they will discharge me and they will not be interested in what happens to me. They kind of dehumanise you in many respects. But they also have a lot of power over you. It comes in different ways, like you know, they do what they want to your body at any time but also you have to eat all your food and there are no negotiations. It's like you've signed over all your control of things…besides you know we don't have a choice of food. You eat what is given to you. (Jon, male, 31)

I should point out here that the depersonalisation and institutionalisation do not take place separately; rather, these occur synchronously in the clinical trial process. Dealing with the changes associated with becoming institutionalised made the participants start to think of the institutional explanations in an attempt to make sense of certain rules and actions that were being imposed on them. This relates to Schutz's view that the relevances and subsequent actions people take can also be imposed. Coming to terms with rules such as 'you must finish the food given to you', regardless of whether they liked it, the participants found themselves thinking of the reasons, or interpretations, of why the research team would impose such rules. The participants generally took a non-questioning and noncritical approach to dealing with the situation and became resigned and compliant.

> The food was absolutely awful. I wouldn't give that food to a dog, but I couldn't question that. I thought maybe it was part of the trial or that surely they wouldn't give us such food for no reason. They must have had a logic for that. (Sasha, female, 27)

> I did not understand why I couldn't be allowed to access my makeup or such small things. I thought maybe it was safety, but it was really bad. But I thought they had a rational reason for that. It's stupid, thinking about it now. (Martha, female, 28)

These quotes illustrate the institutional nature of the clinical trial unit. The participants had to obey the rules or risked being excluded from the trial and subsequently forfeiting their payments. Some participants were shocked by this shift in the way they were perceived. One participant who had experienced an illness which required medication from the GP was eliminated from the trial. Instead of receiving sympathy from research team, they were displeased that their trial data and results had been affected.

> They were not pleased that I had fallen ill and [was required] to take antibiotics and therefore I could not be allowed to take part in the trial. It meant that they couldn't get their results...You could see the disappointment on their faces because I was going to drop out of the trial...no sympathy for me at all. These doctors, they are looking for results. They are paid for their results and so the focus is on the results, and by that I mean positive results, and so they will not tolerate anything that will spoil their outcomes. Otherwise, their product will not go to the market. (Jodie, female, 26)

This quote and preceding discussion illustrate how by taking part in clinical drug trials, healthy volunteers became valuable data for the research. In doing so, they are subject to rules, regulations, and study regimes that ensured the data were not compromised, which is of interest to the institution. This also relates to Marx's observations that the exchange of labour power in value creation often involves those with means of production having power over those they employ to produce value. This is despite the fact that in the contractual negotiations those employed tend to see themselves as free, rational, and with labour power. The irony here is that despite these challenges, some healthy volunteers still repeatedly take part in clinical drug trials.

Healthy Volunteer Redefined: Negotiating Personal Interest and Company Procedures

While volunteering often implies willingness and selflessness, participants felt the selflessness aspect was taken to a new level when they were admitted into a clinical trial. The changes in the way they were viewed by the research team gave the volunteers different ideas of what it means to be a good volunteer. For some, being a seasoned volunteer meant being able to put up with the situation and its consequences. For some, changes in the way they were treated were seen simply as risks of the trade. Healthy volunteers tended to look down on fellow participants who were, in the words of one, 'fussy about things'. Participants who insisted on better treatment found themselves isolated while their colleagues simply got on with being trial subjects.

> I just couldn't cope with her [talking about another HV]. She was always bitching, moaning, whining, and complaining about everything 6 to 6. We had a few words...because you see, if someone decides to come on a trial you must be ready for what it brings. (Ed, male, 28)

The 'ideal' volunteer, therefore, was one who could cope with the situation without feeling inconvenienced by aspects of the clinical trial. A lack of reaction to the challenges was seen as mark of experience in doing clinical drug trials. This is linked to Lyng's (2009) view that in society today risk-taking is viewed in a positive light or even as normal. Of interest is how being in such situations produced different types of agency among volunteers. Some questioned the rules and restrictions; others accepted the status quo. Most participants were aware that there were forums for airing grievances, but they believed that their complaints would be ignored because the staff members to whom they would complain were responsible for administering the trial. In Schutz' terminology, the topical and motivational relevances of the staff were seen to be protecting the interests of the companies they worked for:

> Let's face it here, their aim in the trial is to pass the drug and market it to make money from it...others [staff] are absolutely obsessed with their positions of power. They are, like, this is a scientific trial...they didn't care what you felt...some staff did make sure you felt that way. If I met some of them in my life outside of the trial, I would have words with them.

> I would say, 'That was not acceptable, the way you treated me or spoke to me'. The thing with the trial is that they do dehumanise you...and that is very painful to take. (Sasha, female, 27)

It was clear to many participants that they had become valuable objects of research even while they were devalued as human beings. The participant's view that they would have a word with one of the researchers outside of the clinical trial is very telling; the power context of the trial prevented the participant from airing those views during the trial itself. Some participants said the research teams had downplayed volunteers' unpleasant experiences because it was bad for business to have documented evidence of complaints or extreme side effects.

> They said that: 'Okay, tell us if it gets worse'...they said they'll keep a close eye on you and they said, 'We will look at you'. They try as hard as they can to keep the trial going because if they do tell this [about side effects] the trial may be cancelled. If not, I mean, they can't stop trials going bad—you know, it may hurt their business or profits. (Bob, male, 26)

Staff members were often seen to come up with 'tactics' to keep the trial on track, as Sasha found when experiencing side effects:

> They tried to explain what we were feeling, saying it was psychosis and that's what the psychiatrist on the ward said to us. So I was like, confused, because we went in there without any such problems and when we felt the drug effects, we were diagnosed with psychosis. I think it was a tactic for them to try and ignore the effects we were feeling ...and if they can try and explain away as much as possible of the side effects, they may then continue to the next stage, because if they report extreme effects they may have to stop the trial. (Sasha, female, 27)

The complex nature of the power relations that healthy volunteers have to negotiate in clinical drug trials is clear from the foregoing extracts. The process of becoming a 'data point', involves depersonalisation and institutionalisation coupled with the loss of control or power over what happens to their bodies. The healthy volunteers lose their identities, becoming mere research data, yet valuable assets on whom the progress or failure of the trial depended. The extracts also show the power that staff in the clinical trial units wield over the volunteers and how this contributes to maintaining a total institution.

Market Exchange?

As the participants' value in the eyes of the trial team changed, some of them came to see their involvement in clinical drug trials as a market exchange. By market exchange, I mean that the healthy volunteer's body is exchanged for monetary reward offered by the CROs. For the healthy volunteers, the motivation for taking part in clinical trials is the financial reward, while the corporate motivation or interests were the value of these participants for research and the profits that success of the trial represented. The 2011 Nuffield Report on body part donations is explicit about the economic and symbolic value of the phase 1 clinical drug trials. In addressing the role of healthy volunteers, the report talks of mutuality in the exchange between volunteers and CROs: both parties benefit from the relationship. The report recognises that volunteers have a significant role and acknowledges that they have an interest in the result of the research. However, the emphasis in the report is on how acts by healthy subjects taking part in clinical drug trials are voluntary. By invoking voluntarism, the report and common wider policy debates assume healthy participants act out of altruism. However, as Cooper and Waldby (2014) observe, human involvement in clinical drug trials is part of the 'bio-economy' and healthy volunteering is a form of labour, although it is not usually considered as such by the professionals in the industry. In interviews, the participants in this research demonstrated an acute awareness of how their involvement in clinical drug trials was, in fact, an exchange. They spoke of how the value and nature of the exchange in clinical drug trials were made explicit during the trials.

> It's part of the things you sign up for and I am aware of what is being used of me and I am aware of what I am taking away from them. So I was equally aware of the fact that it's some kind of a transaction here. (Sasha, female, 27)

The volunteers were well aware of the nature of the contract they had agreed to. Answering questions about their motivations, participants were unequivocal in stating their involvement was purely for financial than altruistic reasons. They talked of being unwilling to take part if no rewards were on offer. At the same time, the participants understood that their involvement centred on an economic exchange: their bodies for money. That their bodies were being 'used' denoted not simply a function but also exploitation for the purpose of obtaining results. For the volunteers, the 'use' of their bodies would not be permitted without any compensation.

Healthy Volunteering as 'Passive' Labour

For some participants, healthy volunteering was just like doing any other job with terms similar to a contract or a quote from a plumber: one is free to accept the quote from workman/woman who offers the best deal. This perception emerged in response to questions about how they saw the risks to their bodies and whether healthy volunteering was like selling their bodies. Both assumptions were seen as misplaced—doing trials was an economic exchange.

> It's like calling a plumber or builder. You call out one, give the job description [and] they are going to give you all the details of what they do and price. Then if you are not happy, you go away. (Sam, male, 30)

Significantly, participants drew on daily discourses in which risk was taken to be an occupational affair and thus acceptable (Lyng 2009). It was also common to hear comparisons of clinical drug trials as work compared to other types of work. Clinical drug trials were seen to be easier and more rewarding than, say, working in Tesco; the challenge was to endure being kept indoors subject to strict rules while giving blood regularly.

> It's easy, you know [pause]. Accommodation is provided and they give you food and pay you for sitting around. So, yeah, it is hard work enduring the needles and all that stuff like bloods [giving blood]. But of course, it's better than working in a bar. You won't get paid that much. (Matt, male, 28)

> You know here you just have to sit or lie on your bed and they pay you, better than stacking shelves in Tesco. It's not actual physical labour, it's more inactive.... (Jodie, female, 26)

It is from the participants' use of expressions such as 'easy', 'sitting or lying on your bed' or 'not physically doing anything', yet earning money and creating value for the pharmaceutical industry, that I derive the term 'passive labour'. The term parallels Marx's concept of the production of value based on the exchange of objects for money rather than on relationships between people (Marx 1961). In this context, participants' accounts point to ways in which their bodies disappeared or become absent. Their views seemed focused on the rewards that volunteering offered while for the researcher, it was about the data and potential that healthy volunteers as data presented. Though most volunteers acknowledged actively looking for clinical drug trials and doing that entirely for the reward on offer, most of the participants regarded themselves, ironically, as experienced rather than as 'professional' volunteers as suggested in Abadie's (2010) work.

> Mwale: Would you describe yourself as a professional volunteer, then?
>
> P: What's the other option? If I am not professional, what am I? Um, not really. If I have to make more money I have to do more trials. I think I am experienced and realistic [about the] risks involved. Of course, the money is important but I think I look at what [of what] they are asking of me. (Chase, male, 33)
>
> Mwale: So seeing the number and frequency of your involvement in clinical drug trials, will it be fair to describe you as a professional healthy volunteer?
>
> Sam: Well, no not really. I am more experienced. I know what it takes and what is required. Yes, money is important but I am not running around looking for trials to make money. That's more like a professional, isn't it? Yes, money is what I do this for but not in that sense, I have a [day] job. (Sam, male, 30)

While it was clear that participants talked of doing clinical drug trials as a result of their socioeconomic circumstances, they still wanted to be seen as principled and in control of their situations, as opposed to getting involved in clinical drug trials without considering the risks involved. They acknowledged the difficulties associated with the exchange entailed in clinical drug trials, such as pain, emotional strain, and powerlessness. The rules are set by the CRO, which has the power, and participants are reminded of it when they complain.

> You see, they tend to think…like, 'We are paying you money and so why are you complaining?' So they do not pay attention to the things that we say. They would say things like, 'This is not a five-star hotel and you are being paid to do this'. (Jon, male, 31)

The last extract reveals pointedly how the participants were put in their place, in a way that suggests bullying to ensure compliance during clinical drug trials.

Bodies as 'Resource'

The economic exchanges entailed in healthy volunteering changed participants' views about their bodies. For some, the body was no longer taken for granted but became a resource that needs special care. This change was exhibited in their efforts to improve their chances of enrolling in the trials and prolonging their participation in them to earn money. Therefore, it was relevant to see their bodies as machines that needed careful maintenance:

> Because I see my body as (a machine), just in case I may need some part oiling, you know, and I wasn't aware of it. (Innocent, male, 24)

> I am a healthy person, you know, but if I look after the body then it's okay. Doing trials has not changed anything but ...I know that you can take this medication and they have side effects, and if they have long-term effects the body can recover and bring you back to where you [were before taking part in the clinical drug trials]. (Jazza, male, 28)

These quotes relate to the concept of 'biovalue' (Waldby 2002) specifically on how the healthy volunteers worked on their own bodies to maintain their value in the context of clinical drug trials. Biovalue becomes explicit in relation to the manner in which the materiality of the body provides possibilities for both individuals and institutions to challenge prevailing ethical, sociological, and legal understandings of the role of the body in medical research. Biovalue is linked to how prevailing sociopolitical economies of the body interact with social conditions to bring about certain forms of agency. It is also connected not only to the biomedical developments from which it arises, but also to socioeconomic status and how this influences the individual's willingness or capacity to engage with risk. For healthy volunteers deep in debt, for instance, it is motivationally relevant to view their bodies as constituting biovalue with earning potential. Many volunteers interviewed for this research saw their bodies as assets that needed to be maintained if they were to make money. They did regular exercise, ate less junk food, and generally changed their lifestyles.

> I don't drink coffee or fizzy drinks. I make sure I eat a lot of fruit and veg and do a lot of exercise, and you know, keep the body free of illnesses, because if I do not get into these trials then I cannot earn the money. So I don't drink any alcohol and I don't take recreational drugs. I tried before in Romania, but you see, I have to look after myself. I think my body is valuable and I am lucky to have this body. (James, male, 26)

> We don't eat KFC anymore. Maybe the first weeks we did, but now it's fresh produce. If we are not fit, they will not accept me at the trial. (Melisa, female, 24)

> I have become more aware now of my health and somehow do pay [more] attention to my body than I did before. You know, when they turned me down it was like an awakening that I needed to change. I am happy to do the trials because I now have health checks and...it does help put things in perspective that the body is me, but much more, if I don't look after it well I cannot make the money that I need, so yeah, my body, I must look after it well. (Sam, male, 30)

It is noteworthy that the body becomes, in Schutz's (1970) terminology, topically and motivationally relevant, as 'capital', often after the individual is turned down for a clinical trial because he or she is not 'fit'. The rejection made the body interpretively relevant; volunteers started to think about their bodies differently, which triggered lifestyles changes in order to make their bodies 'marketable' for exchange in clinical drug trials.

> I was turned down twice because I was overweight and I thought to myself, 'This has to change... even clinical trials won't accept me this is not right.' I started doing exercise and changed my lifestyle really. (Matt, male, 28)

It is remarkable here that the body is a valuable resource not only to the pharmaceutical companies; it is equally so to the individual who embodies and offers it for exchange. However, notice the contradiction: while the volunteers took greater care of their bodies through diet and exercise, for instance, taking part in a trial put their bodies at greater risk. The participants seemed to draw on discourses of risk in everyday life to interpret or explain what they were getting into.

The Body and the 'Price' of Passive Labour in Clinical Drug Trials

While money was the motivation for healthy volunteer involvement in clinical drug trials (Tishler and Bartholomae 2002), monetary rewards shaped and perhaps even distorted the experiences and views of participants in the trials. Due to the monetary reward on offer, the participants lowered their guard against risks and resigned themselves to situations they would otherwise have challenged:

> Money was very important for me. (due to the money on offer)...you start to put up with people not being nice, or if things go wrong you start thinking there must be a rational reason why they are doing this. (Sasha, female, 27)

In addition, being paid also seemed to influence the participants' perception and explanation of the adverse effects or to generally having a negative experience on the trial. Some participants interpreted the payment as a reward for coping with being confined indoors for long periods. Others felt they had no choice but to endure the hardships.

> Money was very important and you cannot deny that, because as you do these things you meet all sorts of people who show you around things and remind you to focus on the money. They [staff] also explain it to you: 'It's just simple, we take a bit of blood and a bit of some examination here and there, and then you get the money.' This looks very straightforward, but it's hard. (Jon, male, 31)

Some participants, observed that the exchange evoked feelings of physical vulnerability and powerlessness. Asked how they felt being on a trial as participants who are empowered to leave when they want to, some participants said:

> I thought about that opposite [of empowerment] really, say feeling vulnerable, for a while. I think volunteering is a kind of violation of your body and you can't really separate it from your body...because that's just me, you know, part of me. (Jodie, female, 26)

> Your body is you, and as a result, you may become very sensitive... but you do feel vulnerable definitely, as your body is fiddled with. (Sasha, female, 27)

The participants seemed to find themselves in a conflict between their decisions to become subjects of the trial and allowing for their bodies to be 'fiddled with' for the monetary reward while struggling to come to terms with the hardships they had to endure. At this point, they seemed to view their bodies as closely linked to their identity. Participants spoke of how they started to redefine their bodies as 'who you are', a self-image that cannot be detached from one's sense and experience of oneself. Though the participants were aware that they were involved in some kind of exchange, part of their struggle seemed to come from contending with the idea of selling something and giving it up completely, and the idea of selling something and yet still possessing it. In a sense, they gave up their bodies for research and yet were still embodied beings with a strong sense of physical embodiment. In everyday life, once items are sold and have new owners, their original owner no longer has any say over what happens to those items, no matter how much the item meant to them. However, with the body in clinical drug trials, healthy volunteers retained a sense of owning their bodies in a form of passive labour. While manual labourers put their bodies to work, volunteers in clinical drug trials see their bodies worked upon as they sit and observe the process. At this juncture, ethics of volunteering come into play as conflicts associated with rights emerge: when does the body in such transactions lose its private dimension and become 'public' or even 'corporate'? While ethical debates mobilise the discourse of 'ownership' and 'right to withdraw' with regard to individuals' bodies in clinical drug trials, the topical and interpretive relevance for most volunteers in clinical trial transactions is to do with the loss of control over their bodies. While they have the right to withdraw from a trial, pulling out can have serious consequences.

> It's all very uncomfortable, erm…very invasive. You know, like the doctors can pick you up, put a needle in you, take your blood and do what they want with you. And you have to comply, because you signed a consent form at the beginning which says you will comply. I mean, obviously you can walk out, but then you lose everything. Like I, erm, withdrew myself from the trial…I didn't receive any compensation for the five days that I did, nothing. (Jodie, female, 26)

This quote illustrates the complex nature of the role of the body in clinical drug trials. Doing clinical drug trials for these participants involved complicated negotiations of power relations. In addition to exchanging the body for money, participants also found that in giving their bodies for research they inevitably gave up control and power over their bodies as they were reduced to objects from which data could be obtained. Although the process is subject to regulation, the exchange is weighted in favour of the research companies—they have the power to set the terms of the exchange.

Being a Vulnerable Research Subject

For some participants the loss of power, vulnerability, and hardship made them compare healthy volunteer involvement in clinical drug trials to sex work. Participants made this comparison of their experience in clinical trials to prostitution on their own accord. They were responding to questions about their feelings on being on clinical trial for their first and subsequent trials.

> But after the first one I had this strange feeling, you know, I felt like a prostitute, because I was feeling like I was using my body, because I felt I was giving my body to someone in exchange for money. (Jon, male, 31)

Such feelings often evoked guilt, and questioning of the 'right' way to make a living. Such feelings were a deterrent for some taking part in regular studies, while others came to terms with it. Feelings of vulnerability prompted Lucy to reflect on issues of identity and the meaning of work. Making her body available for clinical drug trials was at odds with her job as a model and actor, for which the body is equally central in the exchange, although in a different way. What was most relevant for Lucy was the loss of power and control during the clinical trial. Lucy described having a:

> .... Disturbing feeling...like I was sinking low and cheap, like I am going in there, sign off things, take a drug and give my blood, you know, like using my body like a prostitute.

She further talked of questioning what had become of her, asking:

> How cheap am I? Is this what it takes to hire yourself out like that?

Significantly, Lucy's account illustrates the extent of powerlessness and vulnerability experienced by healthy volunteers. Lucy also describes ease with which individuals give away power and control when taking part in clinical drug trials:

> …That you give away [power and control] wilfully, you know, and that's what made this whole experience even worse. Yet despite all that, you sign up for it because you think, here is something I could do to make some money easily and still help someone else. (Lucy, female, 25)

However, for other participants comparing healthy volunteering to prostitution was taking the challenges of clinical drug trials too far. They compared healthy volunteering with work in other settings—in a supermarket or being a miner—and argued that participating in a trial was not comparable to prostitution. While acknowledging how the issues they faced in clinical drug trials could be associated with prostitution, they saw healthy volunteering as a personal choice and believed they knew what was asked of them, while prostitution was seen as beset with gender politics. For instance, Sasha clearly disagreed with the view of taking part in clinical drug trials as akin to prostitution, seeing instead the challenges and feelings of vulnerability in healthy volunteering as normal and part of the clinical trial process as involvement is out of choice. For Sasha, healthy volunteering does

> Not involve a sexual power domination. It's not domination because I am sitting there and interacting with other female doctors and female nurses. There is an invasion of my body, but it's nowhere near that which happens in prostitution, you know. That is about power and control, and the interaction I am having is about resources, money and knowledge. (Sasha female, 27)

However, Sasha acknowledges the complex power relations and rules such as being made to eat up all their food, when to sleep and when to wake, and the tight schedule they are subjected to during this. Such kind of control made most participants associate taking part in clinical drug trials similar to prostitution, but was not considered comparable to what happens in prostitution.

> On the level that my body can be used for, then, yeah, but for me I think we have to be careful about that comparison. The sexuality thing is about the value of oneself and goes deeper for me. (Sasha female, 27)

> [Laughs] No, absolutely not. For me this is a transaction. They know what they are getting from me and I know what I will be getting from them. I understand the similarities [between prostitution and healthy volunteering] in that people resolve to do trials due to their economic issues they face,

which is the same as in prostitution, but for me it's like any other work. People, we use our bodies, don't we? (Sam, male, 30)

It should be noted that most of the participants who spoke of healthy volunteering in positive terms had not experienced unexpected side effects while taking part in clinical drug trials. While others had explanations for the side effects that did occur, and often seemed to accept them simply as occupational risks. The risks and loss of power were therefore not of significance for them as for other volunteers. However, those who invoked the comparison with prostitution had all experienced unexpected side effects, making risks and powerlessness topically relevant and consequently requiring an interpretation. The experience of side effects changed their perception of clinical drug trials.

The economic exchange entailed in healthy volunteering changes the perception of work and the body. The changes give rise to dilemmas associated with the relationship between institutions, market exchanges, and the body. The interview data demonstrate the limitation of the idea of volunteering as freedom to act when applied to healthy volunteering in clinical drug trials. The model is problematic in that there are major power differences at play in the transactions. While participants were clearly aware of the nature of the exchange in which they were engaged and their rights, it is undeniable that professionals and institutions wield the definitive power to control the terms of the exchange and to shape the nature of the exchange itself.

Summary

The preceding discussion illustrates the complex nature of the economic exchanges in healthy volunteer involvement in clinical drug trials. In examining the economic dimension of the exchange in clinical drug trials, it is clear how healthy volunteers entering clinical drug trials have to negotiate a process of commodification (Cooper and Waldby 2014), which included experiences of depersonalisation and institutionalisation. Their experiences are revealing of a clinical drug trials unit as a 'total institutional' characterised by a lack of explanation or communications in clinical drug trials with regards to why rules exist and why the diet may be of a certain standard; for example, that the trial may involve testing for drug and food interactions.

While participants may be aware they are involved in an exchange, the power relations involved and the cost, both psychological and physical, of their involvement, they had to come to terms with the idea of having to sell their bodies and were subject to pain and emotional distress during the trials. Disconcertingly, despite the challenges and pain they endure, they have come to see the risks involved as normal and largely acceptable.

Significantly, most rejected the idea of volunteering for altruistic reasons; rather, they argued, it was purely a market exchange and were motivated by the financial reward offered for participating. They dismissed assertions by a minority of their colleagues that they felt an obligation to volunteer for the good of society. The discussion also shows how the contexts of power and straitened financial circumstances influence individual decisions and behaviour as well their understanding of the institutional structures with which they engage. I demonstrate that the body itself acquires, in Schutz's terms 'topical relevance', as a resource for making a living by taking part in clinical drug trials.

References

Abadie, R. (2010). *The professional guinea pig: Big pharma and the risky world of human subjects*. London: Duke University Press.

Cooper, M., & Waldby, C. (2014). *Clinical labor: Tissue donors and research subjects in the global bioeconomy*. Duke University Press.

Goffman, E. (1961). On the characteristics of total institutions. In *Symposium on preventive and social psychiatry* (pp. 43–84). Available at: http://is.muni.cz/el/1423/podzim2009/SOC139/um/soc139_16_Goffman.pdf.

Lyng, S. (2009). Edgework, risk, and uncertainty. In J. Zinn (Ed.), *Social theories of risk and uncertainty: An introduction* (pp. 106–135). Oxford: Blackwell.

Marx, K. (1961). *Economic and philosophical manuscripts. Eric Fromm, Marx's concept of man*. New York, NY: Frederick Ungar. Available at: http://www.912freedomlibrary.org/custom-1/Economic%20and%20Philosophical%20Manuscripts,%20The%20-%20Karl%20Marx%20(1932)%20BM%20Act%20OEF%209.330.pdf.

Mitchell, R., & Waldby, C. (2010). National biobanks: Clinical labor, risk production, and the creation of biovalue. *Science, Technology, & Human Values, 35*(3), 330–355.

Schutz, A. (1970). *Reflections on the problem of relevance* (R. M. Zaner, Trans.). New Haven: Yale University Press.

Tishler, C. L., & Bartholomae, S. (2002). The recruitment of normal healthy volunteers: A review of the literature on the use of financial incentives. *The Journal of Clinical Pharmacology, 42*(4), 365–375.

Waldby, C. (2002). Stem cells, tissue cultures and the production of biovalue. *Health, 6*(3), 305–323.

CHAPTER 7

Volunteering for Free Is Dead, Long Live Reciprocity? Revisiting the Gift Relationship

Abstract Having critiqued voluntarism and altruism to situate healthy volunteering as an economic exchange and thus a form of labour, I now turn attention to the idea of the 'gift relationship' (Titmuss 1971) as applied to human involvement in clinical drug trials. I engage with literature on alturism in the blood donation context and how it relates to debates on human involvement in clinical drug trials. Arguing that while healthy volunteers gave altruism as their motivation in some cases, it is important for altruism in clinical drug trials to be considered in a critical manner. Appeals to altruism obscure power relations and inequality in clinical drug trials in that volunteering tends to attract people who are in financially disadvantaged situations. The use of altruism as motivation or explanation for involvement in clinical drug trials suggests the availability of willing participants who come forward with abandon to take part. Such a view negates how acts of altruism and voluntarism are shaped by the sociopolitical, sociocultural, and socioeconomic contexts in which they take place and that many healthy volunteers in clinical drug trials are actually coerced to take part in clinical drug trials.

Keywords Volunteering · Altruism · Gift · Clinical drug trials · Healthy volunteers · Involvement

S. Mwale, *Healthy Volunteers in Commercial Clinical Drug Trials*,
DOI 10.1007/978-3-319-59214-5_7

The Gift Relationship Today

Deeply embedded in the discussion about healthy volunteering and other forms of human involvement in medical research is the assumption that participants are altruistic in their actions. Building on this idea, debates tend to take a step further by drawing on Richard Titumss (1971) thesis of a gift relationship in which volunteering for medical research or medical donations are construed as a 'gift' exchange, with underlying altruistic motivations. This view draws on Titmuss's (1971) work on the gift relationship associated with blood donations. Titmuss's theory of the gift relationship is based on a comparison of altruistic blood donations in Britain and paid donations in the US, and the relative success of the systems in promoting blood donation. His thesis addressed voluntarism, demonstrating that voluntary donation of blood in Britain, compared to the commercial approach used in the US at the time in which blood donors were paid, was better as it limited donation of contaminated blood. Titmuss is credited with making an important contribution to policy: an official task force in the US was commissioned to respond to his observations (Oakley and Ashton 1997). Titmuss' second contribution to this discussion was evoking Marcel Mauss (2002) anthropological research on gift giving in which giving of gifts was considered to be central to creating and sustaining social solidarity. Mauss observed that exchanges in some indigenous cultures were not only focused on wealth and property, but that such acts were also exchanges of politeness, which included rituals, banquets, festivals, women and children; thus the gift exchange was obligatory and linked to morals in such societies. In fact the economic nature of gift giving was only one aspect of the gift exchange practice (Tutton 2002; Mauss 2002). Titmuss drew on the sociality of gift exchange to argue that blood donation in Britain, at the time, to could equally be construed as an act of gift giving. Today the concept of the gift relationship is used widely and in many contexts (Komter 1996; Madhavan et al. 1997) including research and policy debates. The term has come to be used synchronously with calls for blood and body parts donations and participation in medical research to give 'gifts' of life.

Tutton (2002) provides a salient critical summary of Titmuss's theory, which is equally useful for this discussion here. Tutton observes firstly, that it is important to note how Titmuss diverted from Mauss's theorisation of gift exchange. For Titmuss, acts of gift giving in blood donations were not bound by the same moral obligations and expectations of reciprocity. In other words, people gave blood out of pure sense of altruism, expecting nothing in return. In doing so, as Tutton shows, Titmuss constructed an 'ideal blood donor', which for him was characteristic of the majority of blood donors in Britain as 'the voluntary community donors' (Tutton 2002: 526). Secondly, it would appear that Titmuss was concerned with questions about what makes a good community and by extension how altruism can be indicative of good community relations (Tutton 2002). Oakley and Aston (1997) argue that Titmuss shifted his focus from the traditional approaches to an analysis of policy focused on the administrative aspects to trying to understand the objectives that underpin different social policies. At this point, Titmuss seems to shift altruism from the individual to how institutions, such as the NHS who have contact with blood donors, should embolden acts of altruism so as to foster good community relations in society (Titmuss 1997).

The shift in the conceptualisation of the gift relationship is of significance as acts of altruism no longer become the domain of willing individuals, but become equally embedded in social policy, institutions, and public discourse of volunteering. As Tutton notes, though in practice the idea of the gift relationship cannot be applied in a literal sense, it 'thus achieved a certain metaphorical resonance as part of a broader political discourse on the values of social equality, altruism and community' (Tutton 2002: 528). Volunteering or gift giving have, over time, become established expectations of citizens to get involved in acts of altruism. The idea of volunteering, often taken to be an act of selflessness, has become a political tool in which volunteering is expected in exchange for citizenship rights and claims to state welfare. Titmuss saw altruism as a virtue of the British welfare system and thus better than the commercialized US healthcare system (Tutton 2002). Therefore, it is clear that acts of altruism and volunteering do need to be seen through a critical lens. This is because, much as individuals may take actions of volunteering as personal acts, they are shaped by the political contexts in which individuals find themselves.

Other criticisms of the gift relationship relate to the way Titmuss portrays acts of altruism as though they are a social and biological need to help, in an essentialist way. He seems to suggest that people have an innate ability or an affinity to want to help. In this way he negates how sociostructural, particularly cultural and political contexts, may shape acts of altruism and volunteering (p. 1996). For instance, my discussion in the previous chapter suggests for some healthy volunteers, altruism is actually not part of their motivations for getting involved in clinical drug trials. In addition, there is the question of the applicability of the concept of gift relationship in traditional societies that are responding to changes brought about by modernity (Mauss 2002; Douglas 1990), to different sociocultural and sociopolitical contexts.

Some work has also challenged the universal way in which the gift relationship has been applied to human involvement in medical research and the wider context in which 'gift' exchanges take place. Bourdieu (1990) and with Thompson's (1991) work usefully draws attention to how the gift relationship creates social ties and obligations similar to economic debt, since once given a gift cannot be returned without causing dishonor. In gift exchanges, obligations and rules are often implicit, and debates about gift giving in human involvement in clinical drug trials do not take into account the expectations or reciprocal nature of gift exchanges. In every culture, exchanges of gifts are governed by rules, some of which may bind people to give something in return; in others, saying 'thank you' may not be seen as an adequate expression of thankfulness. It is possible that in other contexts, receiving a gift makes people begin to feel obliged to reciprocate the gift or gesture. In doing so, the gift exchange becomes an exchange based on benefit, but also fulfilling social norms rather than giving freely. For instance, Douglas (1990) and Weiner (1992) point to ways in which the gift exchange creates enduring commitments symptomatic of principal institutions. Within these institutions, people are implicitly expected and obliged to reciprocate the gift. Giving gifts assumes different meanings, including one in which it is viewed as an imposition to and collusion between those involved in the exchange with some social meaning attached to the exchange. In this way, gift giving does not occur in a vacuum but takes place within a moral space with defined, though often implicit, rules about how people should respond when giving gifts. Any gift giving or acts that break these moral codes are often looked down upon, and only some objects are seen as a gift, which suggests that the focus should be on the subtleties of human relationships and interactions. For instance, one would question whether some of the claims of altruism in patients are sincere, which highlights the moral and political nature of human involvement in medical research and the ethical decisions that have to be made. In addition, blood donations are very different from healthy volunteering in invasive and risky phase I commercial clinical drug trials.

These concern how the limits of personal and, for healthy volunteers, economic interests are to be delineated. The investigative conclusions of the sociological and anthropological literature discussed here indicate a need for an analytical approach that examines 'gift giving' and exchanges (in this case volunteering in clinical drug trials) over time as actions embedded in power and political relations, and not merely focusing on the act of 'gift giving', or volunteering in a clinical drug trial, as a self-contained phenomenon.

Nonetheless the aforementioned limitations have not impeded the influence of Titmuss's ideas of altruism from influencing policy and social discourse. In public and policy discourse, it is common to talk of healthy volunteering as acts of gift giving in a Titmussian sense. In this case, involvement has also adopted a moral dimension, in which not giving is construed as failing to live to these ideals. Moral discourse about human involvement in clinical drug trials is prevalent in the research literature today, such as in debates about donations of organs and blood and, indeed, healthy volunteering in medical research as a 'gift'. The Nuffield Report of 2011 on donations of human body parts, which was strongly influenced by anthropology, also emphasised the role of the gift relationship in healthy volunteering in clinical drug trials. However, it is not only in medical literature and policy that engenders altruism, advertisements for healthy volunteers are equally imbued with assertions of participation as an altruistic act. For instance, an analysis of an advert on the Parexel website reads:

> Volunteer to participate
>
> When you participate in a clinical trial, you are helping advance humanity's journey to new discoveries that may save or greatly improve lives worldwide for decades to come
>
> (*Source* https://www.parexel.com/company/volunteer accessed 17/06/2016)

In healthy volunteer recruitment advertisements, altruism is always given as a primary reason why participants should take part in clinical drug trials. This way of presenting altruism arguably plays a part in shaping healthy volunteer responses when questioned about their motivations. Arguably, presenting altruism in this way can be seen as an attempt to minimise potential conflict between care and research in a caring setting such as a hospital. Therefore, there is need to take a critical view of altruism when given as motivation; to consider how social relations and interactions impact on healthy volunteers' responses to questions about their motivation. In other words, there is a need to explore the context in which this altruism takes place and how it is shaped (Morris and Bàlmer 2006). However, it must be stressed here that I do not in any way disavow the possibility of acts of altruism in people's actions, or that all gifts are given in anticipation of something in return. To the contrary, I suggest that rather than framing all acts of healthy volunteering as purely voluntary and altruistic, there is need for an awareness of the complexities associated with volunteering and acts of altruism in phase 1 clinical drug trials.

From Market Exchange to Reciprocal Relationship?

With regard to healthy volunteers and their motivations for involvement in clinical drug trials, the majority were explicit in stating financial rewards as motivation for taking part in clinical drug trials. A few of the participants in the study gave accounts of volunteering free of payment. For some of these participants it should be stated that they first became involved because they were in financial difficulty, and continued to volunteer when they no longer needed the money. For these individuals, volunteering became a reciprocal relationship rather than a gift relationship.

> Well, depends really. One unit was particularly good to me, you see, when I was in a sticky situation. So, I think if they urgently needed me, I can see what I can do. [It] also depends on my time and work schedule. (Jon, male, 31)

> It depends. Some researchers are good and they were good to me, so if they are doing a study and they said to me, 'We have little money, we can't pay you.' I know them. I would say, 'Yes, I will help you', because they helped me when I had a bad time. They ask you, call you by name and make sure you're okay. (Katya, female, 23)

These accounts are in sharp contrast to the quotes in the previous chapter about economic exchange and unequal power in which participants spoke of feeling exploited. The previous accounts illustrate how power works in subtle ways—rather than overtly coercing participants, making them feel special made them want to come back to 'help'. Most participants continued to volunteer after their financial situations had improved. The positive change in their circumstances brought about a change in their attitude to volunteering. For these participants, volunteering again was a way of thanking the research team that had admitted them to a clinical trial; reciprocity became the motivation. Some participants seemed to feel indebted to the research team for having been 'helped' when they were in financial difficulty. Research teams could be seen as deliberately fostering such feelings.

> They call me and have often told me I am a model volunteer, and they often call me first when they have a new clinical trial and they start recruiting. So I am among the first to know about this [laughs]. (Jayne, female, 26)

Such feelings of loyalty or willingness to cooperate affected how the participants interpreted follow-up calls from the CRO's recruitment teams who checked on their well-being after they had completed a trial. Participants who were invited for another trial were more likely to commit to repeated participation, and some started to think of themselves differently. An invitation to volunteer was seen to come from a trustworthy and caring professional who had their best interest at heart. At this point, lay sources of information were less likely to be used and participants were less likely to research the drugs they would be tested on. In making the participants feel wanted and appreciated, the research team were able to influence the participants' views about volunteering. Some participants talked of the researchers as 'being good to me'. This demonstrates how the relationship between volunteers and researchers changed from an economic exchange to a reciprocal exchange. In many ways it also shows—to use Schutz's terminology,—topical or motivational relevancies—may be imposed by institutions or powerful figures to influence individual agency and explanations.

> I would say that money is not as important as it was before. It depends on how much they would require of me. If it was a day or two or a couple of hours here or there, it is not too bad. I mean for me, at the moment I only have Fridays off from work, so I can't actually take time off to do it. So if they want it to be over a long period of time I would not be able to do it, but if they want to do a couple of hours—Mondays, Wednesdays and Fridays—I would say okay then. So yeah, I would do it as a one-off, but I don't think [I would] do more [laughs]) … more than one, you know. It's time. (Jayne, female, 26).

> Sometimes it depends. If it's a unit where I had good rapport with staff and I have time and they called me for a trial and they are offering little or nothing for a short study, I would say, 'Yes, I can help', because basically they were there for me when I needed help, really. (James, male, 26)

It seemed that the participants interpreted an affirmation of their suitability for the trials as a sign that the research team cared about them, highlighting the complex interplay between the notion of the gift, gratitude and altruism.

> They have called me a few times and actually they have told me I am good and reliable, so I am among the first people they always call to check if I am available for a trial. So it's a good relationship. (Jayne, female, 26)

For some taking part in clinical drug trials was seen as a moral obligation. They viewed volunteering as giving without expecting anything in return. A few participants cited personal beliefs, for example, their opposition the use of animals in developing drugs.

> Yes, because I don't really need the money. In fact, I did it because I am against animal testing [for drugs for humans]. So I thought, if I oppose that then I better just do it myself. (Lucy, female, 25)

> Yes, I can do it for free if somebody asked me to. I mean, my goal is to help people. The money is good, but...someone has to give some [thing] to another without expecting something back. It's my duty, I think, to help. (Hope, female, 34)

The declared willingness of these participants to volunteer without expecting anything in return invokes the concept of the gift relationship. Titmuss' (1971) use of the gift relationship steers away from Mauss' idea of reciprocity and obligation. For Titmuss, the gift relationship is based on giving without expecting anything back. Ironically these participants were not taking part in noncommercial studies, but were involved in commercial clinical drug trials with significant rewards on offer. Their involvement in clinical drug trials is, however, more in keeping with ideas of biovalue (Waldby 2002) and citizenship in relation to social responsibility, in which individuals are expected to give something back to society. It should be noted that those who held such views were in a distinct minority. Of significance here is the need for questioning who owns or from where the term volunteer originates. This is because it is itself an indicator of power relations, as some healthy volunteers seem to incorporate their identities in healthy volunteering. Most of the healthy volunteers laughed at the idea of volunteering without being paid; some even questioned the sincerity of those who claimed to be volunteering for the good of society. Responding to my probing as to whether they take part in clinical trials for altruistic reasons, Sam responded:

> We all do this for the money, I don't know anyone who would do it for free. (Sam, male, 30)

Similarly, Chase retorted:

> If anyone says they do it for free it's a ... lie...everyone does it for the money, me included. (Chase, male, 33)

Further, bringing into question the applicability of Titmuss's ideas of gift relationships in British society. Therefore, there is need to consider how altruism and volunteering can become acceptable and expected acts for certain groups to perform. There is need to consider how the advancement of altruism and doing good as a virtue in human involvement in clinical, wraps acts of voluntarism in a veneer of acceptable moral acts. In doing so, altruism and volunteering become interwoven as one and thus removed from the critical scrutiny to which they should be subject.

Healthy Volunteering: Moral Responsibility and Biological Citizenship

The term 'moral' is used here to refer to a common social understanding of what is right and wrong, rather than the meanings governed by ethical principles common in academic discourse. I draw on Zigon (2009: 81), who identifies 'three different, but interrelated, spheres: (1) the institutional, (2) public discourse, and (3) embodied dispositions.' Institutional morality refers to rules and definitions of right and wrongs by social structures and institutions. These institutions in one way or another define whether an individual's behaviour is right or not. Here we could include bioethics and medical ethics as part of institutions that define morality of human behaviours. Linked to institutional conceptions of morality, and yet different, is public discourse. Public discourse refers to morals as defined and used in social interactions in everyday life between people. It also includes public beliefs and understanding of right and wrong that may not necessarily directly be prescribed by institutions, for instance, instructions from parents or literatures. However, institutional and public discourse influence, support, and give credibility to each other, yet the two categories can also undermine each other. Public discourse of morality is also contradictory and diverges, at times starkly, from prevailing institution prescriptions of moralities of society. Public morality also is linked to a third category of morality as habitus. Unlike the idea of morality as prescribed by institutions, often considered to be sentient reflection and rule bound, morality as habitus is not thought through but is merely performed or done. Morality as habitus refers to our embodied dispositions in which everyday actions are unreflective and can be habitual too (Schutz 1970). Morality as habitus is a product of interactions, practice, and experience in everyday life (Zigon 2009). Unlike Bourdieu's concept of habitus linked to socioeconomic status, morality as habitus draws more on the unreflective everyday life and its experiences, which forms the stock of knowledge through which beliefs are acquired and enacted, such as knowledge gained from family and wider social interactions in society. Therefore, as Zigon (2009) suggests, ethics is when the three aspects mentioned earliere interact to shape individual understandings of the rightness or wrongness of their actions. Of course one or two of these aspects may play or a take on a more influential role than the other(s).

Returning to the discussion on human involvement in clinical drug trials, questions about morality can be seen in two ways: first, as moral dilemmas about the use of the human body for medical research in relation to socially acceptable ways of using the body to make a living. In this case, moral questions are asked of healthy volunteers who get involved in clinical drug trials for money. Second, is the question of whether human involvement in clinical drug trials concerns the responsibilities of all citizens. In this section, I will discuss these two questions and conclude with the implications for human involvement in clinical drug trials.

Moral Responsibility or Irresponsibility?

There has been much debate among ethicists and sociologists as to whether it is right or wrong to invite and pay volunteers for participation in clinical drug trials. In the discussion on economic exchanges and the role of the body in Chap. 2, I drew on Scheper-Hughes (2000) and Sharp (2000) to illustrate the moral implications of the use of human subjects in medical research. The moral implications are not about the choice some people make to take part in clinical drug trials, but rather about the fact that involvement in medical research for the reward on offer seems to attract people who are financially disadvantaged. In this context, the question is whether it is degrading to allow humans to subject themselves to such trials in order to make a living. The question draws on sociocultural stipulations which define acceptable and unacceptable activities in which individuals may be involved (Zigon 2007). Sex work is a related area and is shown to attract stigma and labels of recklessness and carelessness (Cobbina and Oselin 2011). Other studies point to ways in which inequality, poverty, and intergenerational disadvantage in society results in certain people being driven to sex work and, indeed, healthy volunteering, to make ends meet (Kempadoo 2003; Sanders 2005). The risky nature of clinical drug trials means that volunteers are sometimes seen as desperate and reckless people seeking quick rewards rather than doing a 'normal' job, and their rationality and morality, like those of sex workers, are often brought into question. Therefore, healthy volunteering and sex work present an opportunity to question the meaning of 'normal' jobs, especially in a neoliberal market economy. In addition, in relation to Titmuss' idea of the gift relationship, one would argue that gift giving then becomes clearly established as a moral act.

Among health volunteers and in reference to risks and work, questions about selling their bodies prompted them to ask what was meant by 'work'; their interpretation of healthy volunteering as being like any other work conveyed adequate motivation to take part. The participants questioned prevailing assumptions and expectations about employment—that 'good work' involves working in an office or conforms to what society defines as a normal job. In addition, some forms of labour such as sex work attract forms of stigma, as they are seen as immoral or reckless. For some participants in this research, the general perception was that all forms of work involved selling one's body in the form of labour in that it involves the notion and reality of exchange as well as the use of the body, though in different ways.

> You know, people think being a volunteer is easy. That pisses me off a lot because it's really 'hard work' [raises fingers to indicate inverted commas]. You have to put up with a lot of stuff, you know, like the needles and

> discomforts, and it's just demanding being woken up at odd hours. It's just like work, you know. (Sam, male, 30)

Reviewing the respondents' reactions to difficult situations reveals how their actions are shaped by normative conceptions about unacceptable responses. Some saw their attempts to find jobs as a response to social definitions of acceptable sources of income and taking part in clinical drug trials as morally suspect:

> Mwale: Are you saying they [parents and family] were morally judging you?
>
> Innocent: You can see how that was linked to work and what they thought was good use of my time … [they] were sort of anxious that I was putting myself in harm's way by doing clinical drug trials and not looking for a 'normal' job.
>
> I just felt violated…what's worse I couldn't tell anyone I was doing trials, I just didn't want anyone to know, because they think I am just careless or not keen on getting a job. (Zara, female, 29)

These comments link concepts of morality and motivation to what society deems acceptable ways of making a living (Forsyth and Deshotels 1998). Taking part in clinical drug trials is considered to be something that reckless individuals do; however, for most of the respondents, taking that step was difficult. This challenges common perceptions of volunteering as dubious morality and risk-taking behaviour. I have to take us back to the idea of 'look at me' with which I opened the book, when my informant invited us to look at her. The invitation 'look at me' also implies there is something shameful about being a volunteer when one has a master's degree, confirming that healthy volunteering in clinical drug trials is done because of circumstantial pressures. Furthermore, the bidding 'look at me' also seems to suggest the individual feels this should not be happening to him/her or that people who share their characteristics do not normally take part in risky behaviour. However, more importantly, the invitation 'look at me' demands that we move beyond a focus on stereotypes associated with social class origins, educational attainment, and social status and identity in order to understand why people take part in clinical drug trials. It is here, therefore, that morality and social justice as part of healthy volunteering become evident. This is because the motivation for engaging with risk can become embedded in cultural practices; over time, the moral lens becomes the 'normal' lens through which engaging with risk in clinical drug trials or similar risky work is viewed. This makes it easy to ignore the wider context in which such actions and behaviours take place by shifting responsibility solely to the individual.

In a way, views on healthy volunteering in today's society relate to Scott's (1977) idea of moral economy. His work draws attention to the need of poor peasants to produce enough to support their families while meeting the social expectations of their society and the risks they take in order to survive (Edelman 2005; Daston 1995). Scott explored the struggles of peasants during years of famine in Burma and Vietnam in the 1930s when they demanded access to land, the right to glean on farmlands, and fair market prices. A parallel can be drawn with the ways in which people are living on the margins in the UK today. Social expectations can influence how people respond to social problems such as unemployment, loss of jobs, or even relative poverty. Questions about healthy volunteering therefore are taken to be ethical questions about how institutions use human subjects in medical research, asking whether it is right to encourage people to engage with risk by paying them huge sums. But the morality of healthy volunteers is also often questioned by society: as illustrated in Chap. 6, their willingness to subject their bodies to such risks for the monetary reward offered is regarded as reckless and irresponsible acts. For others, healthy volunteers are lazy and looking for quick ways to make easy financial gains.

Biological Citizenship?

Social scientists Petryna, Rose, and Novas also examine the moral aspects of taking part in medical research: not only the rights or wrongs about the use of the body in this context, but also how the moral obligations of citizenship have come to include what they call 'biological citizenship'. The meaning of citizenship, they argue, has broadened to include not only civic duties, but also issues to do with the biological reality of human beings, whether as individuals or as members of communities (Petryna 2004; Rose and Novas 2004). Petryna's anthropological study considers the Chernobyl incident and how it shaped the survivors' experience of citizenship with regard to their claims to biomedical resources and justice. The research also looks at how at-risk populations are created through scientific discourses and institutions. For Rose and Novas (2004), biological citizenship stirs a collective sense of community in terms of support for people's rights to treatment and pooling of information. At the individual level, they merge their knowledge about their biological being, resulting in widespread individual acts of personal responsibility to support or even help others. In relation to healthy volunteering, the term 'volunteer' is associated as an act of kindness by citizens to help future patients. To that end, bioethicist Harris argues participation in clinical drug trials is everyone's duty (Harris 2005). His argument is linked to views about volunteering in medical research as a 'gift' and citizens' responsibility. According to this view, volunteering is seen as a social good and of benefit to everyone. However, being involved in clinical drug trials can mean individuals are stigmatised as reckless, as illustrated below:

> My brother said that I was putting money over safety, that I love money too much—why am I putting my life at risk? (Jon, male, 31)

> My mum said, 'Don't be stupid, it's a silly idea. It's reckless. You will make yourself ill and there is no need for you to do that'. …In a way there was an undertone that I should do something productive with my time [rather] than getting myself involved in clinical drug trials. 'Get a job or something'. (Innocent, male, 24)

Others, such as Harris, clearly see it as a noble thing to do and that it should be mandatory. However, participation in some less risky trials—particularly later-phase studies for patients seeking treatment for long-standing illnesses—are considered particularly noble and socially acceptable. Despite this being the case, phrases such as 'helping future populations and patients' are common in recruitment advertisements as demonstrated earlier in this chapter. In this way, it would appear that altruism is clearly used to engender healthy volunteering. Seen this way, biological citizenship as a concept sits well with ideas of 'gift giving', in a Titmussian sense. In this case, healthy volunteering in clinical drug trials is seen implicitly as a characteristic of good citizens. Linked to citizenship, volunteering takes on the meaning of a moral duty, something done for the betterment of society, an attitude that is seen to be a motivation for taking part in clinical drug trials (Almeida et al. 2007; Hallowell et al. 2010) in Titumss' terms of the gift relationship. In this way, the healthy volunteer body becomes a national resource. This raises questions about the uncritical use of the terms 'altruism' 'volunteer', or 'gift giving' in phase 1 clinical drug trials.

The problem with the view of the body as a national resource and volunteering for drug trials as a citizen's duty is that it overlooks the circumstances in which such acts of citizenship are practiced and how people are motivated to take on such a duty. For instance, patients take part in clinical drug trials because they are looking for a solution to their health problems; healthy volunteers participate mostly for monetary gain, as has been illustrated. In other contexts, if volunteering is construed as social good and a duty, it is then undermining the notion of volunteering in such trials. Furthermore, benefits of drugs trials are not always enjoyed equally by citizens. For instance, involvement in clinical drug trials in developing countries where later phase trials are carried out, on drugs intended for Western markets, further illustrates the limitations of embedding voluntarism and citizenship. Petryna (2004) Rajan (2006) and Shah (2006) show how people who are poor or unemployed are more likely to be research subjects in trials whose findings do not benefit them. In such instances, issues of inequality and marginalisation are inevitably raised.

Biological citizenship is linked inextricably to biology and human worth, and unequal experiences are often brought to light. The different ways in which biological citizenship is experienced are reflected in discussions about the importance of human bodies to science and about citizenship among healthy volunteer populations, specifically the political representation of minority racial groups. Epstein (2008) examined how participation in medical research is a political issue in the US, while Pollock has explored the racialisation of drug development in the US and questions the scientific justifications for targeting racial groups in drug development (Pollock 2008). In the UK, Tutton has looked at the inclusion of ethnic minority groups in genetic research (Tutton 2007; Tutton 2009; Tutton and Prainsack 2011). Though this present discussion does not focus on issues of race, it is an important aspect of human involvement in clinical drug trials that is worth discussing in a conversation about phase I clinical drug trials as well. Therefore, a debate on healthy volunteers' experiences as citizens should consider how society, medical research institutions, and governments may harness the discourse of altruism and volunteering as concepts to engender compliance of those volunteering in clinical drug trials, as can be seen in clinical trial advertisements as referred to earlier in this chapter. There is need for an awareness on how understanding of voluntarism and altruism in a Titmussian approach can create a sense of duty to others, to family relations, and the community leading to lack of critical questioning on why some people decide to take part in clinical drug trials. Biological citizenship, therefore, can act as both a coercive tool and a normalizing tool as individuals begin to conform to the norms and expectations of wider society while seeing taking part in clinical drug trials as a normal way of making a living.

Summary

The discussion in this chapter has demonstrated the implications for an emphasis on altruism and volunteering in clinical drug trials. Specifically, I have argued that while claims to altruism may be common in clinical drug trials, there is need to take a critical view of the terms with regard to meanings, and how, where, and why they are used. This is because acts of volunteering take place within a political context in which volunteering as a concept is hijacked culturally and politically to influence people's actions. In other words, a critical approach to understanding altruism and volunteering is needed to take into account the role that social relations and the political contexts shape people's actions. The discussion and findings provide an opportunity to unpack the terms 'altruism' and 'volunteering' further to consider their complexity. This is because to volunteer may not always necessarily imply volitional selfless acts, but reflects how citizenship can be broadened beyond civil rights and duties to include forced or exploitative use of the bodies of the disenfranchised or financially disadvantaged groups in society. In this case, we need to consider how the concepts of altruism, volunteering, and citizenship obscure the inequality and disadvantage experienced by those who may engage in such acts specifically in clinical drug trials. This chapter also highlights the contradictions of everyday morals and institutional ethics, in which certain acts of volunteering or altruism are seen to be moral and thus acceptable—for instance, later phase studies—while early phase clinical drug trials may be seen as reckless acts. This is not an attempt to undermine the significance or indeed availability of altruism and volunteering in society; rather, I suggest a critical engagement and use of these terms to take into account issues of power, inequality, and politics in human involvement in clinical trials.

References

Almeida, L., et al. (2007). Why healthy subjects volunteer for phase I studies and how they perceive their participation. *European Journal of Clinical Pharmacology, 63*(11), 1085–1094.

Bourdieu, P. (1990). *The logic of practice*. Redwood City, CA: Stanford University Press.

Bourdieu, P., & Thompson, J. B. (1991). *Language and symbolic power*. Cambridge, MA: Harvard University Press.

Cobbina, J. E., & Oselin, S. S. (2011). It's not only for the money: An analysis of adolescent versus adult entry into street prostitution. *Sociological Inquiry, 81*(3), 310–332.

Daston, L. (1995). The moral economy of science. *Osiris, 10*(January), 2–24.

Douglas, M. (1990). *"Forward" the gift: The form abd reason for exchange in archaic societies (Trans. W.D Hall)*. New York: W.W Norton.

Edelman, M. (2005). Bringing the moral economy back in...to the study of 21st-century transnational peasant movements. *American Anthropologist, 107*(3), 331–345.

Epstein, S. (2008). The rise of recruitmentology: Clinical research, racial knowledge, and the politics of inclusion and difference. *Social Studies of Science, 38*(5), 801–832.

Forsyth, C. J., & Deshotels, T. (1998). The occupational milieu of the nude dancer. *Deviant Behaviour, 18*, 125–142

Hallowell, N., et al. (2010). An investigation of patients' motivations for their participation in genetics-related research. *Journal of Medical Ethics, 36*(1), 37–45.

Harris, J. (2005). Scientific research is a moral duty. *Journal of Medical Ethics, 31*(4), 242–248.

Kempadoo, K. (2003). Globalizing sex workers' rights. *Canadian Woman Studies, 22*(3), 143–150.

Komter, A. E. (1996). Reciprocity as a principle of exclusion: Gift giving in the Netherlands. *Sociology, 30*(2), 299–316.

Madhavan, S., et al. (1997). The gift relationship between pharmaceutical companies and physicians: An exploratory survey of physicians. *Journal of Clinical Pharmacy and Therapeutics, 22*(3), 207–218.

Mauss, M. (2002). *The gift: The form and reason for exchange in archaic societies*. London: Routledge Classics.

Morris, N., & Bàlmer, B. (2006). Volunteer human subjects' understandings of their participation in a biomedical research experiment. *Social Science and Medicine, 62*(4), 998–1008.

Oakley, A., & Ashton, J. (1997). *The gift relationship: From human blood to social policy*. London School of Economics and Political Science (LSE). http://www.cabdirect.org/abstracts/19972005696.html.

Pollock, A. (2008). Pharmaceutical meaning-making beyond marketing: Racialized subjects of generic Thiazide. *Journal of Law, Medicine andethics, 36*, 530–536
Petryna, A. (2004). Biological citizenship: The science and politics of Chernobyl-exposed populations. *Osiris, 19*(January), 250–265. doi:10.2307/3655243.
Rajan, K. S. (2006). *Biocapital: The constitution of postgenomic life*. Durham: Duke University Press.
Rose, N., & Novas, C. (2004). *Biological citizenship*. Oxford: Blackwell.
Sanders, T. (2005). *Sex work*. London: Routledge.
Scheper-Hughes, N. (2000). The global traffic in human organs 1. *Current Anthropology, 41*(2), 191–224.
Schutz, A. (1970). *Reflections on the problem of relevance* (R. M. Zaner, Trans.). New Haven: Yale University Press.
Scott, J. C. (1977). *The moral economy of the peasant: Rebellion and subsistence in Southeast Asia*. New Haven: Yale University Press.
Shah, S. (2006). *The body hunters: Testing new drugs on the world's poorest patients*. New York: New Press.
Sharp, L. A. (2000). The commodification of the body and its parts. *Annual Review of Anthropology, 29*(1), 287–328.
Titmuss, R. (1971). The gift of blood. *Society, 8*(3), 18–26.
Titmuss, R. M. (1997). *The gift relationship, from human blood to social policy*. New York: The New Press
Tutton, R. (2002). Gift relationships in genetics research. *Science as Culture, 11*(4), 523–542.
Tutton, R. (2007). Constructing participation in genetic databases: Citizenship, governance, and ambivalence. *Science, Technology, & Human Values, 32*(2), 172–195.
Tutton, R. (2009). Biobanks and the inclusion of racial/ethnic minorities. *Race/Ethnicity: Multidisciplinary Global Contexts, 3*(1), 75–95.
Tutton, R., & Prainsack, B. (2011). Enterprising or altruistic selves? Making up research subjects in genetics research. *Sociology of health & illness, 33*(7), 1081–1095.
Waldby, C. (2002). Stem cells, tissue cultures and the production of biovalue. *Health, 6*(3), 305–323.
Weiner, A. B. (1992). *Inalienable possessions: The paradox of keeping-while giving*. Univ of California Press.
Zigon, J. (2007). Moral breakdown and the ethical demand: A theoretical framework for an anthropology of moralities. *Anthropological Theory, 7*(2), 131–150.
Zigon, J. (2009). Developing the moral person: The concepts of human, godmanhood, and feelings in some Russian articulations of morality. *Anthropology of Consciousness, 20*(1), 1–26.

CHAPTER 8

When Human Beings Become Guinea Pigs

Abstract In this concluding chapter, I present the overall argument of this book. My discussion in this book situates human involvement in clinical drug trials in the institutional and sociopolitical, socioeconomic, and sociocultural context that shapes human participation in medical research. This approach has been useful in developing a nuanced understanding of the policy context and the experiences of healthy volunteers in phase I commercial clinical drug trials. Contextualizing the topic in this manner brings about an understanding of healthy volunteers as subjects capable of resisting and negotiating complex and often conflicting socioeconomic and sociopolitical milieus in clinical drug trials. In this chapter, I review the discussion generated so far on healthy volunteering in the UK, and I draw out the implications of the research. These reviews center on the adequacy of existing regulatory structures in protecting healthy volunteers, and how risk in clinical drug trials is perceived by the actors.

Keywords Rationality · Healthy volunteers · Volunteering · Clinical drug trials · Involvement

RATIONAL CONSENT, TRUST, AND RISK

In Chap. 2, I began by considering how sociologists have studied rationality, drawing on the work of Wynne (1996), Horlick-Jones (2005), and Kemshall (1998), among others. My contention is that while such

S. Mwale, *Healthy Volunteers in Commercial Clinical Drug Trials*,
DOI 10.1007/978-3-319-59214-5_8

studies have attempted to understand how people make decisions and view risk in uncertain situations, bioethical conceptions have been influenced by conceptions of individuals as rational actors. Sociological discussions have drawn attention to the ways in which individuals are not always seen to make rational decisions as they are embedded in a social setting. Instead, their decisions, which might as well be rational, are often contingent on the context and situations in which they find themselves. Within bioethics, which is shaped by liberal assumptions of individualism, the principles of autonomy, capability, and rational consent are seen as a necessary process and part of human involvement in clinical drug trials (Wolpe 1998). Despite many sociological and bioethical debates questioning the suitability of such assumptions of rational consent, consent based on the provision of information is central to the policies guiding human involvement in clinical drug trials. The consequences of the dominance of bioethics are illustrated in the discussion about the social context in which individuals make decisions to engage with risk. There is need to consider how factors such as relationships of power and trust and the socioeconomic context, often featuring debt, unemployment, and even homelessness, shape healthy volunteer involvement in clinical drug trials. As discussed in Chap. 2, the bioethics model negates how these factors shape risk perceptions and decision-making. Clearly, within the bioethical understanding of rational consent, there is little consideration of the underlying social processes and how they influence reasoning (Kleinman 1999). I drew on sociological and anthropological research into human involvement in clinical drug trials to illustrate how these contexts shape decision-making. Substantive research and policy debates in this area has tended to focus on the issues arising out of the role of patients as research subjects in clinical drug trials—their responses, experiences, and views, and questions of diagnosis and treatment—with little focus on the needs and experiences of healthy volunteers. This attitude has tended to suggest that patients and healthy volunteers have the same needs and ethical concerns when, in fact, they do not. Rather, consideration of healthy volunteer involvement in clinical drug trials should be seen in the context of socioeconomic and the sociopolitical inequalities in which such acts take place, taking into account how structural inequalities and power may shape and facilitate acts of voluntarism and attitudes to risk.

The Volunteering Turn and Its Policy Implications

I introduced this book with a description of the background leading to the development of healthy volunteering in clinical drug trials. I considered the commercial and regulatory context in which clinical drug trials take place, and how this is linked to the growth of the pharmaceutical industry; public demands for cheaper, better, and safer medicines; and the government's provisions to balance support for industry with adequate regulation and ethical oversight. In the discussion, I highlighted how regulation of human involvement in clinical drug trials is influenced by utilitarian ethics and a rational conception of human subjects as capable of representing their own interests. In the context of an increase in clinical drug trials and the growth of the pharmaceutical industry, healthy volunteers have become a valuable resource for pharmaceutical corporations. In neoliberal terms, the state facilitates such growth under the banners of individual liberty and the free-market economy, while volunteers are exposed to exploitation in an unequal engagement with powerful organisations and institutions. To ardent rational choice theorists and advocates of liberal economics, healthy volunteers are rational, willing, and capable beings, and possibly even entrepreneurs taking their initiative in using their bodies to make a profit. Socially and culturally, healthy volunteers can be seen as reckless individuals. However, conceiving healthy volunteering in this way is problematic, as it negates the complex situations people find themselves in when they decide to take part in clinical drug trials. In many ways, the emphasis on the terms 'volunteer' and 'altruism' obscures inequality in healthy volunteering; it is only sensible to see people who resort to healthy volunteering as people in financial challenges trying to get by. This is not to suggest that healthy volunteers do not make rational decisions, but rather that these decisions may also be irrational or indeed shaped by the political and institutional contexts in which they find themselves. Therefore, ethical considerations need to move beyond the simple cost–benefit analysis of decision-making by taking into account how power, trust, and socio-economic and socio-political situations influence decision-making. In taking into account the everyday taken-for-granted experiences and accounts, space is provided for a critical view and use of the terms 'healthy volunteer' and 'altruism' in research and policy discourse, while acknowledging the significance of such acts of voluntarism and altruism to society. There is need for a policy and regulatory framework that deals with such challenges effectively and transparently. Consideration should be given to how business and healthcare priorities have undue influence on human involvement in clinical research and the role and experience of healthy volunteers. On the policy front, as illustrated in the discussion in Chap. 2, legal and policy frameworks promote autonomy of individuals and markets to protect the safety of human volunteers in clinical drug trials, improve healthcare for the public, and foster business growth. However, pharmaceutical corporations do not necessarily share these commitments to the wider public good (Goldacre 2012; Rajan 2006) .

The Limits of Rational Consent

I have shown how policy discourse tends to present healthy volunteers as being positioned outside commercial transactions; it overemphasizes altruism and voluntarism as motivations, as shown in the Nuffield Report (2011), despite the highly commercialised context of clinical drug trials. My discussion, drawing on Petryna (2005), (Fisher 2009), and Cooper and Walby (2014), who allude to the commercial and political contexts in which value is created in medical research and the practical challenges they bring, has highlighted that healthy volunteers need more protection than the industry offers. Discussions about regulation and safety centre on the notion of rational consent and the need to protect patients, children, and those considered mentally incapable of making rational decisions. There is also a tendency to conflate volunteers with patients, whether they are involved in routine healthcare or clinical drug trials, and to see the provision of adequate information as the solution to any ethical dilemmas that might arise in clinical drug trials. However, there is little understanding that the vulnerability of participants might well extend beyond matters of physical and mental health to include the socioeconomic and sociopolitical contexts in which they live. I draw on the conceptions of vulnerability of Fineman (2008) and look beyond the medicalised policy definition of vulnerability associated with victimhood or pathology. I argue for the need for a broader view of vulnerability that challenges the idea of a capable, independent, and liberal subjects. Specifically, in reference to healthy volunteers, consideration should be given to their financial difficulties, the social attitudes they contend with, and their routine interactions with professionals that influence their encounters with risk. This raises two important questions. First, if the regulatory framework ensures that individuals take responsibility for their decisions, will it be clear when things go wrong in clinical drug trials that they were deemed capable of giving rational consent? Second, what should be made of the uncertainties surrounding healthy volunteers' consent for the use of their bodies in clinical drug trials?

The problems raised by the volunteering in clinical drug trials of individuals who are financially needy or desperate and who may not fully understand—or if they do, may ignore—the risks are not resolved in existing policy and regulatory frameworks. Regulation should take into account the diverse social circumstances and the interactions in which consent is given. On another level, the challenge is to ensure a viable commercial milieu which establishes commercial phase I trials as legitimate and facilitates the flourishing of science and industry to meet public expectations of better healthcare. The problem is that there is a tendency to position healthy volunteer involvement as existing outside of, and separate from, the commercial domain. While the potential for exploitation is acknowledged, monetary reward for participation is seen as compensation for volunteers' inconvenience, discomfort, and time in the trials. I argue for a discourse of policy on human involvement in clinical drug trials that addresses not only compliance with regulations, but also the need for a deeper understanding of how and why individuals decide to take part in clinical drug trials in the first place, and whether they bear too much responsibility for the risks they take. The policy and regulatory framework in the context of commercial and increased human involvement in clinical drug trials should consider the wider social context and the complex nature of the exchanges, the body in trials for the monetary reward on offer, to guide human involvement in clinical drug trials.

Motivations: Altruism or Economic Exchanges in Clinical Drug Trials?

In this discussion, I contend that monetary rewards are the primary motivation for volunteers. Generally, healthy volunteers' decisions to get involved in clinical drug trials were influenced by their social circumstances such as excessive debt, unemployment, and inadequate incomes. For most healthy volunteers, taking part in clinical drug trials was seen initially as a last resort or a one-off commitment to address an immediate financial need. Many became repeat volunteers, usually after incident-free trials and interactions with supportive staff. Participants also tended to feel that they owed researchers something in return for helping them when they were having financial problems the first time they volunteered. As a result, they expressed willingness to come back and volunteer even if, in some cases, it was free of payment or for reduced pay. A minority of volunteers cited altruism as a motivation; for these participants involvement in clinical drug trials was aimed at contributing to society. Others, motivated by monetary rewards, tended to justify their participation in ways that implied social acceptability. The term 'volunteers' was found to be qualified by the complex social and financial circumstances and power relations in which the individuals found themselves. However, I have illustrated in the discussion the limitations of an indiscriminate use of the terms volunteering and altruism in healthy volunteer clinical drug trials. I have shown how the use of such terms tends to neglect the power relations, the obligations, and the expectations that may be placed on people to volunteer or indeed to do good to benefit society.

In the discussion, I have shown how ideas of citizenship today mean that to claim welfare and rights people may be expected to volunteer. In Chap. 1, I gave an example of an employment advertisement which categorized healthy volunteering in clinical drug trials as a permanent job. In Chap. 7, I have gone further to illustrate how evoking altruism and volunteering in the form of the 'gift relationship' neglects the sociopolitical context of acts of altruism. My concern is that such a view ignores how human involvement in commercial phase I clinical drug trials is closely linked to new forms of citizenship and shaped by social and moral expectations of citizenship, which, in turn, influence public views and experiences of medical research. Rose and Novas's (2004) concept of biological citizenship was shown to have resonance for human involvement in clinical drug trials. Current developments, such as the UK government's growing support for the pharmaceutical industry in the development of science and improved healthcare delivery (Will 2011), and the creation of the Biobank (Tutton 2009; Mitchell and Waldby 2010), are examples of ways in which citizenship is being reconstituted to focus not only on civil rights but also on the biological aspects of citizenship. In this context, the focus is on the duty of citizens to contribute to the development of science for the betterment of societal health. The discourse of healthy volunteering as a gift relationship has thus flourished. However, assumptions of how biological citizenship and gift relationships work in practice preclude wider discussions about individual and social moral reasoning and the milieu in which gift relationships and biological citizenship take place.

Healthy Volunteering as 'Passive Labour'

Rather than seeing volunteering as mere acts of benevolence by individuals to help society, sociology needs to analyze critically how such acts take place. Specifically, it is important to consider the complex sociopolitical, sociocultural, and socioeconomic contexts in which people 'volunteer' and how these shape views and legitimize risk-taking for certain groups. For instance, the unseen, and often unconsidered by the public, neoliberal forces that shape volunteer recruitment and interactions between the public and commercial medico-technological innovations contribute to how the public view their bodies in their engagement with risk. Bodies have become tools that are used to make a living by taking part in clinical drug trials for significant rewards on offer from the research companies. Important contributions have been made to this discussion by Fisher (2007), Elliott (2008), and Abadie (2010); their works have explored how socioeconomic and sociopolitical forces influence healthy volunteer involvement in clinical drug trials in the US. However, both in the US and in the UK, official government regulatory—specifically bioethical—and industry discourse has situated healthy volunteering as being mainly altruistic and voluntary. Human involvement in commercial clinical drug trials involves an economic exchange of the body. The healthy volunteers I interviewed were highly aware of the nature of the exchanges they were involved in and explicit about how they felt about the process. Some of the participants who talked of healthy volunteering as an exchange compared it to prostitution: a straight exchange of the body for money. However, the discourse of altruism and volunteers seems convenient in policy and industry discourse, as it makes it possible on one hand to render invisible the inequalities associated with the business of clinical drug trials, but on the other to make clinical drug trials impossible to scrutinize. Therefore, in cases where trials have gone wrong, it is easy to think of those affected as either selfish and thus not worthy of our sympathy, while on the other hand, it can be said that those who take part in clinical drug trials are rational and thus responsible for their actions.

Arguably, healthy volunteering has parallels with emerging research interests in surrogate mothers (Waldby and Cooper 2008; Cooper and Waldby 2014). The exchange in clinical drug trials is what I call 'passive labour'. Accounts of such passive labour have parallels with Waldby's (2004) concept of 'biovalue' and 'clinical labour', in which biological products attain value in medical research. The healthy volunteer participants in this research saw a need to work on their bodies to maintain their value, even if they did not use the term 'biovalue' to describe it. Significantly, it is how participants in clinical drug trials see their involvement, on one hand, as any other kind of work, while, on the other hand, as easy, since they do not have to do anything such as manual labour to produce value but 'just lie'. The relationship to Marx's idea of the fetish and production of value is also useful here. Parallels can be made with Marx's idea of lack of means of subsistence and how it relates to involvement in exploitative labour relations. While participation in clinical drug trials attracts people from a variety of backgrounds, it is the shared lack of means of production, or being in a financially straitened situation, that both groups share that is of significance here. In clinical drug trials, it is the bodies of people in financial disadvantage who are more likely to take part as volunteers, while for Marx those lacking the means of production are usually the poor or proletariats (working classes). While traditional labour forms involved physical manual labour, passive labour involves the body as a site on which value is created; in this case, participants do not have to do anything but 'be there' as their bodies do the work in the form of metabolising the trial drug and giving of body fluids such as blood. Observations and analysis of the body and body fluids, respectively, results in the generation of valuable data for the research companies, while healthy volunteers are paid substantial sums for their involvement. All this illustrates how healthy volunteering is a form of labour for people in straitened financial situations.

Re-Reading Schutz: System of Relevances and Human Involvement in Commercial Phase I Clinical Drug Trials

Turning to Schutz's (1970) system of relevances as a conceptual tool for explaining human involvement in clinical drug trials, introduced in Chap. 3, I critiqued bioethics and rational choice theory for emphasizing rationality and capability in the decision-making process, noting that it is contingent upon issues of trust and power which individuals must negotiate. The idea of rationality fails to consider behaviours that may be habitual and thus undertaken without much prior thought. In addition, it overemphasizes ability and choice. To understand healthy volunteering better, therefore, requires a framework that offers a wider view of human involvement in clinical drug trials, one that considers restrictions and resistance alongside rational and irrational, active and passive aspects.

It is against this background that I adopted Schutz's phenomenology of system of relevances in explaining human involvement in clinical drug trials. The theory focuses on actions or behaviours that are often overlooked, and in doing so explores taken-for-granted behaviours—what Schutz refers to as the 'world of routine activities' (Schutz 1970:139). Although Schutz has been criticised for his reference to a philosophy of consciousness, for being overly subjective, and for ignoring individual interactions with structures, power, and how these constrain human behaviour (Goettlich 2011), the concepts he introduces add to our understanding of this broader terrain of decision-making. Firstly, rather than locate decision-making as purely based on cognition, Schutz situates decision-making as a social process as well, and one that is thus amenable to sociological analysis. Secondly, decision-making is then seen to be based on more than just a cost–benefit analysis, but embedded in social relations, experiences, and knowledge as well. And thirdly, using this approach illustrates how social structures influence decision-making, since individuals are located in conflicting and powerful political interests which shape relationships and decision-making. These theoretical tools help to analyse institutions, power, individual decision-making, and a range of social contexts.

The significance of exploring human involvement in clinical drug trials becomes clear when we consider what Schutz calls 'intrinsic' and 'imposed' relevance. By this he means the ways in which relevances can be experienced as internal or imposed by external factors, such as laws or prevailing attitudes in society, or as voluntary or involuntary. Imposed relevances can also refer to the institutional context in which agency takes place—the rules, customs, and values and the wider political milieu, including the capitalist economy—and how they shape how we experience and feel about ourselves and the choices we make.

Turning to the data on healthy volunteering, I have argued that the system of relevance provides a tool for explaining healthy volunteers' decision-making. Few of them had considered taking part in clinical drug trials; instead, they had done what they could to make a living in more conventional ways, such as getting a job. However, when confronted with mounting bills and excessive debt that could not be dealt with by using conventional means such as finding a 'normal' job or borrowing money, and when presented with an opportunity to take part in clinical drug trials, healthy volunteering became of topical relevance—they had to think of the benefits of this option (in other ways a case of interpretative relevance) and how it could solve their financial problems. This interpretation had to be in keeping with their existing stock of knowledge and yet was also shaped by wider institutional influences, such as the stigma attached to volunteering, the rhetoric of rational consent, trust in institutions, and the idea of the gift relationship and biological citizenship. In sum, these factors could be understood as motivational relevances.

While this applies to healthy volunteers' motivations for taking part in clinical drug trials, the same can be said of their engagement with risk. Some volunteers saw engagement with risk as normal, simply an occupational matter. In this sense, their perception was well within the taken-for-granted realm of Schutz's scheme of relevances, particularly when healthy volunteering became habitual and healthy volunteers became accustomed to the risks. As long as they were confronted with the same stimuli and same processes with the same outcomes, they did not consider the risks to be a problem. In fact, the more often they took part in clinical drug trials, the less inclined they were to question the process. Additional factors, such as the trust they had in the professionals doing the research, provided the basis for the stock of knowledge they had regarding the safety of clinical drug trials. For most of these participants, the issue of risk did not require further investigation or explanation.

However, the meaning of risk changed when trial participants were faced with unexpected side effects. Then they would question the experts who were administering the trial and sought explanations as to what may have gone wrong: an example of interpretive relevance. For instance, Participant 5 talked of asking the researchers for clarity on what was going on, while Participant 29 talked of thinking that there was a rational explanation to the adverse reactions she experienced. Some volunteers assumed there were rational explanations for why certain things were done a certain way. Others who experienced adverse events or had misgivings occasioned by a lack of satisfactory explanations by staff members shunned certain kinds of clinical drug trials or avoided further involvement altogether—an example of motivational relevance.

It is important to note that the decision-making process does not always flow in an orderly manner; rather, it is a fluid process. Some decisions are not just about addressing problems that can be explained, but are also about resisting conventional means of seeing the world. Some volunteers disagreed that their participation in clinical drug trials was reckless; they questioned common attitudes about work and saw their involvement as resembling paid labour, which often comes with risks. While a minority gave personal values and beliefs as their motivation, most cited the desire to resolve personal financial problems.

The 'imposed' nature of these relevances related to ways in which healthy volunteers' involvement was defined and regulated by institutions, which, in turn, enabled and yet constrained agency. Schutz's theory is also useful in analysing institutional policies in showing that power and influence do not rely only on the presence or absence of capability and rationality, but also on the degree to which behaviours and actions are shaped by the 'imposed' nature of the topical, interpretive, and motivational relevances of everyday life. For instance, the labelling and stigma associated with healthy volunteering as an activity undertaken by people who are reckless arises from the differences in the relevances between those who do and do not take part in clinical drug trials. For some, initially taking part in clinical drug trials may not be of high relevance. However, in a society where what you do for a living is a marker of your success in life and reflects your social class and education, taking part in clinical drug trials as a volunteer becomes highly relevant. The supposedly objective interpretation by those who do not take part in clinical drug trials influences one's view of her/himself and defines them as being part of the 'in-group'—in this case healthy volunteers. Schutz's theory offers a tool to analyse the perspectives of the individual who is subjected to prejudice and the institutional context in which healthy volunteering occurs.

The differences in healthy volunteers' attitudes about risk and strategies for dealing with it, as highlighted in this research, can certainly be understood through Schutz's system of relevances. The healthy volunteers who talked of engaging in clinical drug trials without concern for the risks involved could not be distinguished from those who were careful about risks, because of their differences in risk perception but because of the context—specifically, their experiences of adverse effects or financial situation at the time they decided to get involved in clinical drug trials. Although for many healthy volunteers in this research, risk avoidance was topically relevant, they found that their decisions and actions were constrained by the social and institutional context in which decisions had to be made. Those who avoided risks did so by using strategies which gave them control over certain aspects of the process, though only to a limited extent (Bloor 1995).

Understood in this way, healthy volunteering is an engagement with complex power relations in a setting of competing and conflicting personal and commercial interests. It becomes clear that the use of the term 'volunteering' can be misleading and obscure the inequalities that give rise to the exploitation of human beings for the value that their bodies possess. Rather than seeing trial volunteers as reckless individuals, a more nuanced understanding of healthy volunteering would take account of the circumstances and context in which they decide to participate in clinical drug trials.

Therefore, Schutz's theory of system of relevances is useful for exploring the ways in which individuals can reconstitute themselves in responding to their varying financial situations. It was shown that participants in this research, particularly healthy volunteers, recognised their participation in clinical drug trials as a commercial transaction, and they came to view their bodies and themselves differently. How they rationalised the exchange and devised ways of negotiating this complex relationship made it clear that they do not take part in clinical drug trials indiscriminately. On the contrary, their decisions were found to be contingent on several factors that challenge the normalised conceptions of healthy volunteers revealed in Chap. 5, which portrayed them as careless and motivated by a desire to make quick money. In fact, the healthy volunteers' accounts in this book were found to be mostly educated and held well-paid jobs. In view of the discussions in Chap. 6, it appears that healthy volunteering in commercial clinical drug trials provides a space for individuals to experience what it means to have biovalue and to be consumers and participants in the Western neoliberal marketplace as they challenge, resist, negotiate, and exploit the commodification of their bodies in the form of passive labour. In this book, I have highlighted both positive and negative aspects by suggesting that human involvement in clinical drug trials is not done out of an entirely free, unconstrained 'choice', but that it is an outcome of the interaction of personal circumstances with wider sociopolitical contexts which makes individuals get involved as they reflect on their social situations, practices, and relationships within neoliberal capitalist economies.

In summary, using Schutz's understanding of relevances and their role in social interactions allows for a sympathetic concept of healthy volunteers, rather than the common but incomplete portrayal of volunteers as capable, rational subjects or as reckless and greedy. It highlighted ways in which involvement in clinical drug trials gives healthy volunteers space to construct identities informed by a sense of their biovalue. At the same time, Schutz's ideas allow us to take into account how social-institutional relationships influence volunteer involvement in clinical drug trials. Far from seeing Schutz's system of relevances as being entirely subjective, considering the imposed and involuntary aspects of his theory therefore requires considering how the vocabulary of bioethics and corporate interests give rise to the creation of biovalue and sets the terms on which healthy volunteers and corporations interact in clinical drug trials.

Policy Implications: Improving Protection of Healthy Volunteers in Medical Research

Concerning policy actions, I would like to echo some of Abadie's (2010) suggestions. Fistly, there is a need to acknowledge that healthy volunteering is a form of work, which I have called 'passive labour', and thus to ensure the provision of safe and fair working conditions. This should go beyond the system in which consent is given, to clarify the processes for dealing with CROs to prevent bullying or coercion, problems that were described by some participants in this research. A framework in which impartial information and advice are made available to volunteers would be useful. Support services for volunteers in clinical drug trials are provided by the same companies that administer the trials, and it is possible that many healthy volunteers have faced situations they would rather have avoided if they had had adequate representation and impartial advice. Ultimately, healthy volunteers should have a bigger say in important decisions about the ways in which phase I commercial clinical drug trials are conducted and regulated. They have no platform to campaign for better conditions or improved rewards. By contrast, patients are represented by patient organisations and charities who ensure they get a better deal in clinical drug trials.

There is a need for robust discussion among professionals, regulators, and healthy volunteers on how rewards are calculated, to ensure that they are fair and represent good value for the volunteers, rather than leaving it to the industry to determine what to pay. Healthy volunteers should have a means to provide feedback about their experiences in clinical trial units: a web-based platform is one possibility. This could also be a forum to rate facilities and report problems about contracts, for instance, or payments when dropping out of a trial. Follow-up mechanisms after trials could be improved by providing clear guidelines about timeframes and for record-keeping. The MHRA and ethics committees could be responsible for policing this.

A major concern of mine at the beginning of this project in 2008 was the lack of industry consensus on the use of volunteer registers to avoid over-volunteering. Since then the registers have been transferred to the HRA and NRES, but the impact this will have in preventing over-volunteering remains to be seen. Providing an EU-wide register would benefit the industry greatly by helping to ensure that volunteers are not overexposed to certain chemical agents when taking part in clinical drug trials across international boundaries. There is also a need to investigate drug interactions in healthy subjects who take part in multiple studies and the appropriate intervals between studies. At the moment, there is no consensus among experts about drug interactions within this time frame, although 3 months seems to be a standard time limit. Such clarity would help to direct support and information in the right direction, including to human volunteers themselves.

Clearly, the measures proposed here would provide better protection for human subjects in clinical drug trials. But would the pharmaceutical industry support provisions that might affect its business in a system that it regards as adequate? Also, the proposal to give volunteers a greater say in decisions about reward and conditions in clinical drug trials might be difficult to implement, because they are not found in one place; bringing them together, even online, would require a great deal of organisation and mobilisation, although databases now controlled by the HRA and NRES would facilitate such an initiative. Besides, implementing such changes would require substantial funding.

In conclusion, it is only appropriate to return to what my intentions were in putting this book together. My aim is to bring about debate that would lead to a reconsideration of how healthy volunteering in clinical drug trials is conceived by the different professionals involved, and the public in the UK. I opened with an anecdote of one my participant's invitation to 'look at me'. It is common to see healthy volunteering as an activity that is done by people out there or indeed in far-off places, and thus does not concern us. However, the risks taken by the individuals who take part in clinical drug trials benefit us all, whether with regard to health or indeed as professionals mediating the development and use of medicines; thus we are all implicated in clinical drug trials. It is easy to dismiss or even ignore the humanity associated with clinical drug trials and focus instead on the technical processes; after all, healthy volunteering in the eyes of utilitarian ethicists is framed as an act by rational and consenting individuals. In this context, information provision is considered to resolve ethical dilemmas that may result from human involvement in clinical drug trials. However, there is more at play than what is presented commonly in theoretical and policy debates as 'rational consent' and 'information provision'. In fact, the significance given to rational consent and information provision as demonstrations of capability for healthy volunteer involvement in clinical drug trials results may be inadvertently obscuring inequality and disadvantage experienced by individuals who take part in clinical drug trials as healthy volunteers. In addition, a focus on consent and rationality tends to situate healthy volunteering as apolitical, negating the complex political and social context in which acts of healthy volunteering take place.

Therefore, if we want to avoid a repeat of events—such as those in Rennes in January 2016, where involvement in clinical drug trials led to a death of a healthy volunteer while leaving five others in a critical condition; or indeed closer to home; in Northwick Park in London 2006, where healthy volunteers suffered life-changing adverse effects—there is a need to reconsider how healthy volunteering is framed and viewed. Note that these examples are events that capture media attention; however, responses to the aftermath of such disasters all have in common a tendency to make the participants who suffer the consequences become hidden and forgotten until another similar disaster happens again. However, the experiences and accounts of healthy volunteers in the discussion generated so far—such as Asha, who was forced to take part in clinical drug trials under existing regulatory frameworks—exemplify the need for a critical unpacking of 'volunteering' to reveal the humanity, inequality, and powerlessness that some healthy volunteers experience, and the inadequacies of existing regulatory frameworks to offer adequate protection to healthy volunteers in commercial phase I trials.

Drawing on Simone Weir's observation, there is no injustice greater than to suggest that the experiences of healthy volunteers do not interest us. We need to develop an awareness of and focus attention on the complexities associated with acts of volunteering. By this I mean, we need to start by asking what we mean by volunteering in clinical drug trials, and how in casually using the term 'volunteer' we contribute to maintaining the status quo in which inequalities present in healthy volunteering are simply swept aside as acts of rational, consenting individuals. This is not to suggest people cannot volunteer or that people are incapable of altruism, but rather that we need to take a critical look at the ways in which the concepts are used. Taking a critical perspective of volunteering bids for different kinds of relationships with people around us, developing and asking a wider range of questions and problems (Back 2015) resulting in a rethinking of what we mean by 'volunteering' itself.

We need to reflect on the complexity and the sociopolitical nature of human involvement in clinical drug trials. It is ironic that sociology has not until the recent past seriously explored healthy volunteer involvement in clinical drug trials. We need to connect with the approaches suggested by Schutz (1970), Black (2015), and Plummer (2013) in which sociological attention is paid to everyday taken-for-granted social interactions. Doing so helps bring to the fore complex forms of inequality and going into details to explore how what may flippantly be dismissed as acts of a few reckless or lazy individuals in the eyes of others or acts of 'rational actors' can bring to life everyday experiences of debt, low pay, and increasing cost of living. In looking at healthy volunteer involvement in this way, a considered sociological understanding of human involvement in clinical drug trials is developed. Such a sociological view has as at its root questions of inequality and justice, and framings of motivations, demographics, and rewards in commercial phase I trials when human beings become guinea pigs.

References

Abadie, R. (2010). *The professional guinea pig: Big pharma and the risky world of human subjects.* London: Duke University Press.

Albertson Fineman, M. (2008). The vulnerable subject: Anchoring equality in the human condition. *Yale JL & Feminism, 20*, 1.

Back, L. (2015). Why everyday life matters: Class, community and making life livable. *Sociology, 49*(5), 820–836.

Bloor, M. (1995). *The sociology of HIV transmission.* London: Sage.

Cooper, M., & Waldby, C. (2014). *Clinical labor: Tissue donors and research subjects in the global bioeconomy.* Duke University Press.

Elliott, C. (2008). Guinea-pigging: Healthy human subjects for drug safety trials are in demand. But is it a living?. *New Yorker (New York, NY: 1925)*, 36–41.

Fisher, J. A. (2007). Coming soon to a physician near you: Medical neoliberalism and pharmaceutical clinical drug trials. *Harvard Health Policy Review: A Student Publication of the Harvard Interfaculty Initiative in Health Policy, 8*(1), 61.

Fisher, J. A. (2009). *Medical research for hire: The political economy of pharmaceutical clinical drug trials*. New Brunswick, NJ: Rutgers University Press.
Goettlich, A. (2011). Power and powerlessness: Alfred Schutz's theory of relevance and its possible impact on a sociological analysis of power. *Civitas–Revista de Ciências Sociais, 11*(3), 491–508.
Goldacre, B. (2012). *Bad pharma: How drug companies mislead doctors and harm patients*. London: Fourth Estate.
Horlick-Jones, T. (2005). Informal logics of risk: Contingency and modes of practical reasoning. *Journal of Risk Research, 8*(3), 253–272.
Kemshall, H. (1998). *Risk in Probation Practice*. Aldershot: Ashgate.
Kleinman, A. (1999). Moral experience and ethical reflection: Can ethnography reconcile them? A quandary for 'the new bioethics'. *Dædalus, 128*(4), 69–97.
Mitchell, R., & Waldby, C. (2010). National biobanks: Clinical labor, risk production, and the creation of biovalue. *Science, Technology, & Human Values, 35*(3), 330–355.
Nuffield Council on Bioethics. (2011). *Human bodies: Donation for medicine and research*. London: Nuffield Council on Bioethics.
Petryna, A. (2005). Ethical variability: Drug development and globalizing clinical drug trials. *American Ethnologist, 32*(2), 183–197.
Plummer, K. (2013). Epilogue: A manifesto for a critical humanism in sociology: On questioning the human social world. In D. Nehring (Ed.), *Sociology: An introductory textbook and reader* (pp. 498–517). Harlow: Pearson.
Rajan, K. S. (2006). *Biocapital: The constitution of postgenomic life*. Durham, NC: Duke University Press.
Rose, N., & Novas, C. (2004). *Biological citizenship*. Oxford: Blackwell Publishing.
Schutz, A. (1970). *Reflections on the problem of relevance* (R. M. Zaner, Trans.). New Haven: Yale University Press.
Tutton, R. (2009). Biobanks and the inclusion of racial/ethnic minorities. *Race/Ethnicity: Multidisciplinary Global Contexts, 3*(1), 75–95.
Waldby, C., & Cooper, M. (2008). The biopolitics of reproduction: Post-Fordist biotechnology and women's clinical labour. *Australian Feminist Studies, 23*(55), 57–73.
Will, C. M. (2011). Mutual benefit, added value? *Journal of Cultural Economy, 4*(1), 11–26.
Wolpe, P. R. (1998). The triumph of autonomy in American bioethics: A sociological view. In R. DeVries, & J. Subedi (Eds.), *Bioethics and Society: Constructing the Ethical Enterprise* (pp. 38–59). New Jersey: Prentice Hall.
Wynne, B. (1996). May the sheep safely graze? A reflexive view of the expert-lay knowledge divide. In S. Lash, B. Szerszynski, & B. Wynne (Eds.), *Risk, environment and modernity: Towards a new ecoclogy*. London: Sage.

References

Abraham, J. (2008). Sociology of pharmaceuticals development and regulation: A realist empirical research programme. *Sociology of Health & Illness, 30*(6), 869–885.

Abraham, J., & Lewis, G. (2000). *Regulating medicines in Europe: Competition expertise and public health.* London: Routledge.

Adam, D. (2006). Why use guinea pigs in animal testing? *The Guardian, The Science Behind the News,* available at https://www.theguardian.com/science/2005/aug/25/thisweekssciencequestions1.

Anonymous. (1747). *Adventures of the kidnapped orphan.* London: M. Thrush.

Bendelow, G. A. (2006). Pain, suffering and risk. *Health, Risk & Society, 8*(1), 59–70.

Bentley, J. P., & Thacker, P. G. (2004). The influence of risk and monetary payment on the research participation decision making process. *Journal of Medical Ethics, 30*(3), 293–298.

Booth, R. (2017). £1.74 an hour: Jinn couriers complain over low earnings. *The Guardian.* Retrieved February 13, 2017, from https://www.theguardian.com/business/2017/feb/13/125-for-72-hours-work-jinn-couriers-complain-over-low-earnings?CMP=oth_b-aplnews_d-2.

Deshotels, T., & Forsyth, C. J. (2006). Strategic flirting and the emotional tab of exotic dancing. *Deviant Behavior, 27*(2), 223–241.

Dickert, N. W. (2013). Concealment and fabrication: The hidden price of payment for research participation? *Clinical Drug Trials, 10,* 840–841.

Fisher, J. A., & Kalbaugh, C. A. (2012). Altruism in clinical research: Coordinators' orientation to their professional roles. *Nursing Outlook, 60*(3), 143–148.

Haynes, P. (2015). *Managing complexity in the public services.* London: Routledge.

S. Mwale, *Healthy Volunteers in Commercial Clinical Drug Trials,*
DOI 10.1007/978-3-319-59214-5

Hochschild, A. R. (1983). *The managed heart.* Berkeley: University of California Press.

Hornblum, A. M. (1998). *Acres of skin: Human experiments at Holmesburg Prison: A true story of abuse and exploitation in the name of medical science.* New York: Routledge.

ICH Harmonised Tripartite Guideline. (2009). *Nonclinical Evaluation for Anticancer Pharmaceuticals S9.* International Conference on Harmonization.

Johnston, L., & Longhurst, R. (2009). *Space, place, and sex: Geographies of sexualities.* Rowman & Littlefield.

Keynes, J. M. (2006). *General theory of employment, interest and money.* Atlantic Books.

Leder, D. (1990). *The absent body.* University of Chicago Press.

Lemmens, T., & Elliott, C. (1999). Guinea pigs on the payroll: The ethics of paying research subjects. *Accountability in Research, 7*(1), 3–20.

Marx, K. (1887). Capital: A critique of political economy. In *Book one: The process of production of capital* (Vol. 1) (S. Moore, E. Aveling, & F. Engels, Trans.). Moscow: Progress Publishers.

Milgram, S. (1963). Behavioral study of obedience. *The Journal of Abnormal and Social Psychology, 67*(4), 371.

Moser, D. J., et al. (2004). Coercion and informed consent in research involving prisoners. *Comprehensive Psychiatry, 45*(1), 1–9.

Mwale, S. (2015). *Risk, rewards and regulation: Exploring regulatory and ethical dimensions of human research participation in phase i (First-in-Human) clinical drug trials in the United Kingdom.* Brighton: University of Sussex. University of Sussex Library Archives.

O'Neill, O. (2003). Some limits of informed consent. *Journal of Medical Ethics, 29*(1), 4–7.

Pescosolido, B. A. (1992). Beyond rational choice: The social dynamics of how people seek help. *American Journal of Sociology, 97*(4), 1096–1138.

Roberts, E. F. S., & Scheper-Hughes, N. (2011). Introduction: Medical migrations. *Body & Society, 17*(2–3), 1–30.

Royal College of Physicians. (1986). *Research on healthy volunteers,* 20: 243–257.

Shaw, B. G. (1913). The quintessence of Ibesenis–Now completed to the death of Ibsen, The University Press Cambridge, available at http://www.rosings-digitalpublications.com/shaw_george_bernard_1856_1950_quintessence_of_ibsenism.pdf.

Spivak, G. C. (1985). The Rani of Sirmur: An essay in reading the archives. *History and Theory, 24*(3), 247–272.

Thompson, E. P. (1971). The moral economy of the English crowd in the eighteenth century. *Past and Present, 50,* 76–136.

Wallace, A. (2012). "Feels like I'm doing it on my own": Examining the synchronicity between policy responses and the circumstances and experiences of mortgage borrowers in arrears. *Social Policy and Society, 11*(01), 117–129.
Watson, J. J. (2003). The relationship of materialism to spending tendencies, saving, and debt. *Journal of Economic Psychology, 24*(6), 723–739.
Weil, S. (1977). *The Simone Weil reader.* New York: Dorset Press-, University of Michigan.
Weinstein, M. (2001). A public culture for guinea pigs: US human research subjects after the Tuskegee Study. *Science as Culture, 10*(2), 195–223.
WHO (World Health Organization). (1995). Guidelines for Good Clinical Practice (GCP) for trials on pharmaceutical products. *Technical Report Series, 850,* 97–136.
Wilson, B. (2017). *What is the 'gig' economy?* BBC business news. Retrieved February 10, 2017, from http://www.bbc.co.uk/news/business-38930048.

Websites:

www.myukjobs.co.uk/paid-medical-trials-eczema-sufferers-2506424.
www.quintilesclinicaltrials.co.uk.

Index

S. Mwale, *Healthy Volunteers in Commercial Clinical Drug Trials*,
DOI 10.1007/978-3-319-59214-5